To my dearest Jennifer, without whose constant love and support none of this would have been possible.

Dreamweaver 4/ Fireworks 4

Visual JumpStart

Dreamweaver®4/Fireworks®4
Visual JumpStart™

Ethan Watrall

SYBEX®

San Francisco ◆ Paris ◆ Düsseldorf ◆ Soest ◆ London

Associate Publisher: Cheryl Applewood
Contracts and Licensing Manager: Kristine O'Callaghan
Acquisitions and Developmental Editor: Mariann Barsolo
Editors: Donna Crossman, Pete Gaughan
Production Editor: Nathan Whiteside
Technical Editor: John G. Moore
Book Designer: Maureen Forys, Happenstance Type-O-Rama
Electronic Publishing Specialist: Susie Hendrickson
Proofreaders: Andrea Fox, Amey Garber, Laurie O'Connell, Yariv Rabinovitch, Nancy Riddiough
Indexer: Ted Laux
Cover Designer: Daniel Ziegler
Cover Illustrator/Photographer: Daniel Ziegler

Library of Congress Card Number: 01-086019

ISBN: 0-7821-2832-7

Acknowledgments

This being my first published work, there are quite a number of people who, I think, deserve a word of thanks for their help (either directly or indirectly) in bringing this project to fruition.

Many thanks need to go out to my agent David Fugate of Waterside Productions Inc. I am forever in his debt for all the work, help, and wonderful advice he gave during this project. I certainly hope I'll have his wise counsel for years to come.

At Sybex, Nathan Whiteside, Donna Crossman, and Susie Hendrickson all deserve praise for all of their help and hard work during the later stages of production. Thanks to John G. Moore, my technical editor, for all his hard work. Many thanks to Dan Mummert at Sybex for all the work he did helping me secure copyright permissions for the various screenshots in my color section. Without the help of Mariann Barsolo, my acquisitions editor at Sybex, I can honestly say that this project would have been incredibly more difficult. She was always there with great advice, tons of help, and a level of tolerance for my silly first-time author questions that (at least in my book) should qualify her for sainthood. I'd also like to express my thanks to Pete Gaughan for all of his help during the final stages of the project. Thanks to Rick Schrand for lots of help and good advice as the book was just getting started.

I must offer my gratitude for the help that Pam Statz gave when I was seeking web sites for the color section. A very special thanks to Doug Chiang, who, despite his full schedule, was always willing to answer any questions I threw his way. I must also extend my thanks to the rest of the people who allowed me to include screenshots of their web sites in the color section.

I need to thank my friend Norbert Herber for all of his support and suggestions throughout the project. My longtime friend, Neil Birch, also deserves my thanks for his support and insightful comments. While this will probably make them scratch their collective heads, many thanks to my advisory committee (Dr. Chris Peebles, Dr. Anne Pyburn, and Dr. Richard Wilk) for making it easy for me to write this book. Special thanks to Dr. Jeanne Sept who, when this book was being written, was amazingly tolerant of my somewhat underwhelming contributions to the Prehistoric Puzzles Project. Thanks to my dad, who, besides lots of encouragement and thoughtful advice, never once asked what an archaeologist was doing writing a book about web design. Thanks also to my mom for her support during the project. My love and thanks to Taylor, who thought it was totally cool that I was writing a book and never once complained when I kicked her off the computer because I needed to write.

Finally, my sincere apologies to anyone whom I managed to forget. Thanks everybody!

Contents

Contents

Contents

Introduction

Back in 1989, Tim Berners-Lee of the European Particle Physics Laboratory (CERN) wrote an innocent little document titled *Information Management: A Proposal* that, among other things, outlined the development of Hypertext Markup Language (HTML). Little did he realize that the modest 18-page document would forever change the way in which we access, acquire, and share information.

HTML caught on like wildfire. By July 1993, there were hundreds of computers worldwide that could deliver HTML documents. The world had just gotten a whole lot bigger.

Fast-forward to 1997, when, much to the joy of the web-design community (and the average web user, for that matter), Macromedia Dreamweaver 1.0 was released. No more handwriting HTML, no more puzzling over cryptic lines of code, and certainly no more head scratching for those who weren't trained programmers. Macromedia had unveiled the future, and the future looked good.

While Dreamweaver certainly wasn't the first WYSIWYG (What You See Is What You Get) web-design tool, it was arguably one of the best and brightest. Including such revolutionary features as an intuitive and flexible visual authoring environment, Roundtrip HTML, and support for Dynamic HTML, Dreamweaver was easily one of the most powerful web tools to come down the pipe.

Not long after that, Macromedia, recognizing that the web was becoming a far more visual medium than ever before, announced the release of Fireworks 1.0 in March of 1998. Designed as a tool to provide a unified environment for creating, optimizing, and producing high-quality web graphics, Fireworks inaugurated a new category of authoring tools.

Several years and several versions later, Dreamweaver is arguably the most popular visual web-authoring tool available. With over 700,000 users and a market share of more than 75 percent, Dreamweaver has made high-level web authoring accessible to both professional and amateur designers. Likewise, Fireworks has been widely accepted as the best tool for creating images for the web. In December 1999, Macromedia announced the release of Dreamweaver 4 Fireworks 4 Studio, a software bundle that provided a unified web-design solution for professionals and amateurs alike.

About This Book

The sheer popularity of the web has created a large group of people clambering to get their digital creations out there. It's only natural that many of these people—most of whom have very little experience with computers, let alone web design—would turn to Dreamweaver and Fireworks. This is where this book comes in.

Building on the high standard set by the Visual JumpStart series, this volume provides guidance for green Dreamweaver and Fireworks users as they dip their toes for the first time in the great ocean of information that is the World Wide Web. The strength of the volume rests on its step-by-step approach to the material, as well as the highly visual manner in which the information is presented. It's very important to remember that this volume is designed to serve simply as an introduction to basic (and some intermediate) Dreamweaver and Fireworks features. As a result, the only assumptions made herein are that anyone who chooses to use this book has previously worked with a desktop computer and understands the operational basics thereof.

It's also important to point out that, while all the screenshots used throughout the course of the book are taken from the Windows version of Dreamweaver and Fireworks, Macintosh users won't be excluded. One of the great joys of most Macromedia products (especially Dreamweaver and Fireworks) is that they function almost identically from platform to platform. There are some superficial visual differences (which are a result of the different operating systems and not the programs themselves) and different hotkeys (which will be given in both Mac and Win forms), but Mac users won't have any problems getting the most out of this book.

Note

Hotkeys will always be given for both Macintosh and Windows users, in that order. For example, Opt/Alt+F7 indicates that the Mac shortcut is Option+F7, while the Win shortcut is Alt+F7.

Who Needs This Book?

The most important thing that potential readers of this book should realize is that it is intended solely for those who have very little or no experience using Dreamweaver and Fireworks. Those users who need no introduction to the basics of either program should look elsewhere. I certainly don't want to discourage any interested individual from using this book. Quite the contrary! However,

I feel that users more experienced with Dreamweaver and Fireworks might not find exactly what they are looking for with this title.

Having said that, I would encourage anyone eager to take part in the digital media revolution to read this book! Any students wanting to put their class projects on the web, any new parents wanting to put pictures of their newborn on the web, and certainly any business wanting to set up a digital storefront should read this book. In short, this book is for anyone who is excited about the endless possibilities of the web but is a little befuddled about where they should start.

How This Book Is Organized

There is a natural progression of skills involved in both the creation of a web page with Dreamweaver and the creation and manipulation of an image in Fireworks. The chapter-by-chapter structure of this volume is designed to emulate that progression. While each chapter builds on the previous one to a certain extent, the volume can in fact be used as a reference for those wishing to tackle a specific problem. For the sake of structure, Dreamweaver is discussed in the first part of the volume, while Fireworks is discussed in the latter part.

Here is a quick look at what a reader can expect to explore in each chapter:

Chapter 1   Deals primarily with an introduction to the Dreamweaver environment. Included is a look at the ways in which a user can customize the Dreamweaver workspace. Finally, the chapter deals with the creation of a local site, arguably one of the most important steps in the creation of a Dreamweaver web site.

Chapter 2   Looks at the earliest steps that need to be taken when creating your first web page. Topics include opening and saving a document, setting page properties, and previewing your work in a browser.

Chapter 3   Covers the basics of text creation and manipulation. Users will learn how to change text size, font, and color. Also included are the finer points of text organization, as well as the addition of special characters and spell checking.

Chapter 4   Explores image addition and manipulation. Included is a short, but important, look at web image formats.

Chapter 5 Looks at the lifeblood of the web: hyperlinks. Readers will learn, among other things, how to attach links to text and images, change link color, and create named anchors.

Chapter 6 Covers the creation of tables as well as the finer points of table manipulation.

Chapter 7 Begins our look at Fireworks with a detailed exploration of the program's interface and workspace.

Chapter 8 Deals primarily with the initial creation of a Fireworks document. The chapter also covers opening an existing document, opening multiple documents, and importing image files from other sources.

Chapter 9 Looks at the basic tools and concepts involved with the creation of images in Fireworks. Included is a look at bitmap and vector image-creation and manipulation tools.

Chapter 10 Explores the addition of text to a Fireworks document. Readers will learn how to change fonts, text color, style, and alignment.

Chapter 11 Deals with how users can optimize their graphics for the web. Included is a look at the steps involved in exporting a Fireworks image as a GIF and as a JPEG. Readers will also learn how to use Fireworks's handy Optimization Wizard.

Chapter 12 Caps off our look at Fireworks with an exploration of what it takes to create an animated GIF. Included are the finer points of symbol creation and management, frame additions and deletions, and onion skinning.

Appendix Provides a host of useful and exciting online resources for those who want to expand their newfound knowledge and skills by venturing onto the web.

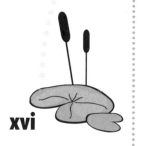

What Isn't Covered in This Book

I feel it's my duty as the author to tell you not only what is covered in the book, but also what was left out. It's my sincere hope that readers will take the information presented in this volume as an introduction to the wonderful world of Dreamweaver and Fireworks. However, I also hope that readers realize that there is a lot more about Dreamweaver and Fireworks that was left out.

These topics are among those not covered on the Dreamweaver side: frames, behaviors, Cascading Style Sheets, HTML styles, animating with the Timeline tool, templates, library items, forms, and layers. On the Fireworks side, Bézier curves, special effects, object transformation, image maps, slices, and behaviors were left out. For those eager to learn these and other more advanced Dreamweaver and Fireworks topics, I recommend picking up a copy of *Mastering Dreamweaver 4 and Fireworks 4* by David Crowder and Rhonda Crowder (Sybex, 2001).

How to Use This Book

This book can be used in two different ways. The first, as mentioned earlier, depends on the fact that the material presented follows a logical learning curve. Someone can easily read the book from cover to cover, confident in the fact that, when they are done, they'll have a solid foundation in the basic procedures of Dreamweaver and Fireworks. The second way that this book can be used is as a reference. Readers looking to solve certain problems or learn specific skills can simply locate the information they desire by using the index or the contents page.

The bottom line is that whichever way readers decide to use this book, they will develop the skills necessary to continue their journey in the wonderful world of Dreamweaver and Fireworks.

Fire up your computers and grab ahold of something nailed down; it's going to be a wild ride!

Making the Most of This Book

At the beginning of each chapter in this book, you will find a list of topics that you will learn in that chapter.

To enhance your knowledge of Dreamweaver and Fireworks, there are key terms that are italicized in the text and also defined within the margins on the book. Text that you type will appear in **bold** font. Monospaced font indicates a web address. The ➤ symbol separates program menu items or Toolbar icons.

You will also find other elements in the text to help:

Note
Notes provide extra information and references to related information.

Tip
Tips are insights that help you perform tasks more easily and effectively.

Warning
Warnings alert you to things you should do—or shouldn't do.

Sidebar

Sidebars enhance your learning by explaining how to take the next step.

How to Reach the Author

I am always interested in hearing readers' comments, thoughts, questions, constructive criticisms, or general musings on the meaning of life. I can be reached through my general correspondence e-mail at ecwatral@indiana.edu. Alternatively, good old-fashioned paper correspondence can be sent to Ethan Watrall, c/o Sybex, 1151 Marina Village Parkway, Alameda, CA 94501.

Part 1

First Steps in Dreamweaver

In this part, you'll start off by looking at Dreamweaver 4's new features. You'll continue by exploring the Dreamweaver interface and customizing that interface. You'll also learn how to set up the initial page properties of a Dreamweaver document. Finally, you'll start building your creation by setting up a local site on your computer's hard drive.

First Steps in Dreamweaver

Chapter 1

Starting Up Dreamweaver

After double-clicking the Dreamweaver program icon, you will be faced with a myriad of windows, palettes, and inspectors. The possibilities are endless. But fear not, fellow traveler, you will become well acquainted with the Dreamweaver environment. Before we get started, however, there are a few things that need to be introduced. First and most important is an introduction to the Dreamweaver environment and the ways it can be molded to suit your preferences. Then, the chapter will close with a look at how to set up a local site on your own hard drive. In this chapter, you will learn about the following topics:

- A tour of the Dreamweaver interface

- Customizing the Dreamweaver environment

- Setting up a local site

A Tour of the Dreamweaver Interface

One of the great joys of Dreamweaver is its interface. The program boasts an incredible set of tools, all of which need to be right at your fingertips at a moment's notice. The interface, which is designed to accommodate a wide range of expertise and working styles, allows you to maximize what's really important—creativity. The interface itself is broken up into a series of windows, palettes, and inspectors. In this section, you'll be introduced to the most common of these tools.

Note

Never a company to do any following, Macromedia has managed to stay well ahead of the pack with this newest release of Dreamweaver. The program itself has some very cool new features that fit into four general categories: code, design, collaborative tools, and user interface. For a more detailed look at Dreamweaver 4's new features, check out the bonus web-only content for this volume at www.sybex.com/2832.

The Document Window

All of your creations will take shape in the Document Window. Think of it as a canvas upon which you paint your web pages. Don't be fooled by its initial emptiness, however. The Document Window is far more than just a vacant space into which you mold your creations. There is an abundance of information and tools built right into the Status Bar, which lies at the bottom of the Document Window. The following subsection will explore the most important of these tools.

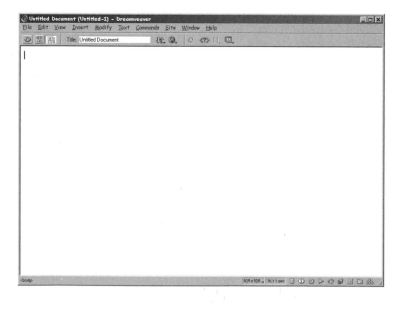

The Tag Selector

The Tag Selector is a nifty selection tool that displays the HTML tags that are associated with any given element you select. Simply click the particular tag of an element, and that element—be it an image, a table, or text—is automatically selected.

Window Size

The Window Size serves two primary functions. First, it provides an indicator as to the current size (in pixels) of the Document Window you're currently working in. Second, if you resize your window, the Window Size changes immediately to reflect the new value. By clicking the Window Size and opening the drop-down menu, you can easily choose from a preset list of window sizes.

Document Size/Download Time

The Document Size/Download Time indicator is one of the unsung heroes of the Dreamweaver environment. Basically, it tells you the current size of your page (in kilobytes) and the amount of time (in seconds) it will take to download it over a 28.8KBps modem connection.

As you add objects to your page, both numbers will increase. If you spend a lot of time thinking about bandwidth, this is definitely a tool to keep your eye on. Later in this chapter, you will learn how to change the reading to reflect the download time at different speeds— over a 56KBps modem or a cable modem, for example.

The Mini-Launcher

With a click of the mouse, the Mini-Launcher allows you to launch (from left to right) the Site Window, the HTML Styles Palette, the Cascading Style Sheet Palette, the Behaviors Palette, the History Palette, the HTML Inspector, and the Assets Panel. A little later in the chapter you'll learn about the Mini-Launcher's big brother, the Launcher, and how you can add and remove tools from the Launcher.

The Toolbar

The Toolbar is a neat tool that is new to Dreamweaver 4 and includes some new features as well as some old ones. The Toolbar lets you toggle between the Code View, the Split View, and the Design View. It also contains a handy field into which you can enter your page title (without having to open the Page Properties dialog box), a button to access the File Status menu (which contains the current state of the file you're working on), a button to launch your target browser, and a drop-down options menu.

The Property Inspector

The Property Inspector is probably the most frequently used tool in Dreamweaver. Essentially, it serves as a doorway to the properties of any given object (be it a table, an image, or a string of text).

Its power lies in the fact that it is a dynamic tool, meaning that the options displayed change depending on what sort of object you select. For example, if you select a string of text, you'll be able to change font, color, and size. On the other hand, when you click a table, you'll be able to change the number of columns or rows, relative dimensions, border thickness and color, and cell content alignment. So, you see, it's a pretty powerful and useful tool. To access the Property Inspector, all you need to do is go to Windows ➢ Properties, or use the shortcut Command+F3 (Macintosh) or Ctrl+F3 (Windows).

Tip

Oftentimes, you can access less common attributes of a given object. To see them, click the expander arrow (the down-pointing arrow in the bottom right-hand corner of the Property Inspector).

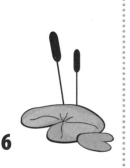

The Launcher

The Launcher, which is the big brother of the Mini-Launcher, allows a quick and easy one-click access to some of Dreamweaver's most widely used palettes and inspectors. Unlike the Mini-Launcher, the Launcher is itself a floating palette. To access the Launcher, go to Windows ➢ Launcher, or use the shortcut F2.

One of the great things about the Launcher (as well as the Mini-Launcher) is the fact that you can customize which tools are visible. To add (or remove) tools from the Launcher, simply follow these steps:

1. Go to Edit ➢ Preferences, or use the shortcut Cmd/Ctrl+U, to open the Preferences dialog box.

2. Select Panels in the Category list box.

3. If you want to add a tool to the Launcher, simply click the plus (+) button next to Show in Launcher and make your choice from the drop-down menu.

4. To remove a tool from the launcher, simply select it from the list next to Show in Launcher and click the subtract (−) button.

Tip

You can change the orientation of the Launcher from horizontal to vertical (and back again) by pressing the repositioning icon (the little rectangle) in the lower right-hand corner.

The Object Palette

Beyond the Property Inspector, the Object Palette is probably one of the most widely used tools in Dreamweaver. By simply clicking one of the icons, it provides a quick and easy way to insert pretty much any object into your document. In Dreamweaver 4, the Layout Mode tools—something we'll discuss in Chapter 6, "Working with Tables"—are accessible at the bottom of the Object Palette. To access the Object Palette, select Windows ➢ Objects, or use the shortcut Cmd/Ctrl+F2.

The Object Palette is actually composed of 7 different panels that contain a group of similar objects.

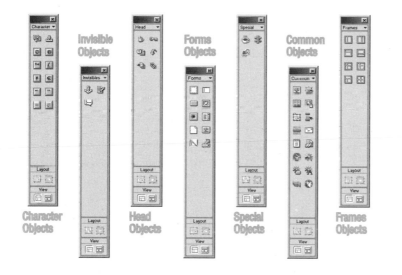

All of the individual panels are accessible through the drop-down menu that is opened when you click the down-pointing arrow in the top right-hand corner of the Object Palette.

Object

Any element (such as a table, image, or Flash text) that is inserted into the Document Window using the Object Palette.

Tip

While the Object Palette is a handy tool, it can often clutter up your working space. In order to maximize your available screen space, simply close the Object Palette and use the Insert menu to introduce objects into your document.

The Assets Panel

The Assets Panel is the best new feature of Dreamweaver 4. As web sites have grown in complexity, managing media assets has become an increasingly daunting task. Any web site can have hundreds of images, audio files, and multimedia files. The Assets Panel provides a quick and convenient way to view all colors, images, external URLs, scripts, Flash files, Shockwave files, QuickTime files, templates, and library items in a central location.

Each asset can be first viewed in the preview window of the Assets Panel and then easily added to your web page by simply dragging it into the Document Window. To access the Assets Panel, go to Window ➢ Assets or use the shortcut F6.

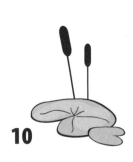

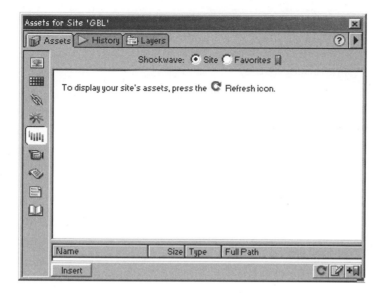

Tip

By clicking the Add to Favorites button in the lower right-hand corner of the panel, you can add assets to a list of favorites that can be reused across any number of local sites.

Warning

Remember that the Assets Panel will work only on a previously defined local site.

Customizing the Dreamweaver Environment

Dreamweaver offers the user the opportunity to deeply shape the interface. In this section, we'll look at some of the more popular ways in which you can customize the preferences in Dreamweaver.

Editing Keyboard Shortcuts

Keyboard shortcuts are a quick and easy way to access a program's functions. Until now, however, most programs only offered the user an immutable set of shortcuts. But Dreamweaver 4 offers a Keyboard Shortcuts editor that allows you to create your own shortcuts, edit existing shortcuts, or choose from the fixed list of shortcut sets included. To access the Keyboard Shortcuts editor, select Edit ➢ Keyboard Shortcuts.

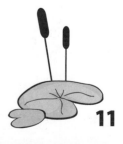

Keyboard Shortcuts

Current Set: Macromedia Standard

Commands: Menu Commands

⊞ File
⊞ Edit
⊞ View
⊞ Insert
⊞ Modify
⊞ Text
⊞ Commands
⊞ Site
⊞ Window
⊞ Help

Shortcuts: + −

Press Key: Change

Help   OK   Cancel

Adding a Shortcut to a Command

To attach a shortcut to a command, simply follow these steps:

1. Go to Edit ➢ Keyboard Shortcuts to open the Keyboard Shortcuts editor.

2. Click the plus (+) to expand the command category (File, Edit, View, Insert, etc.) that you want to work with.

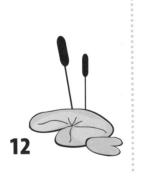

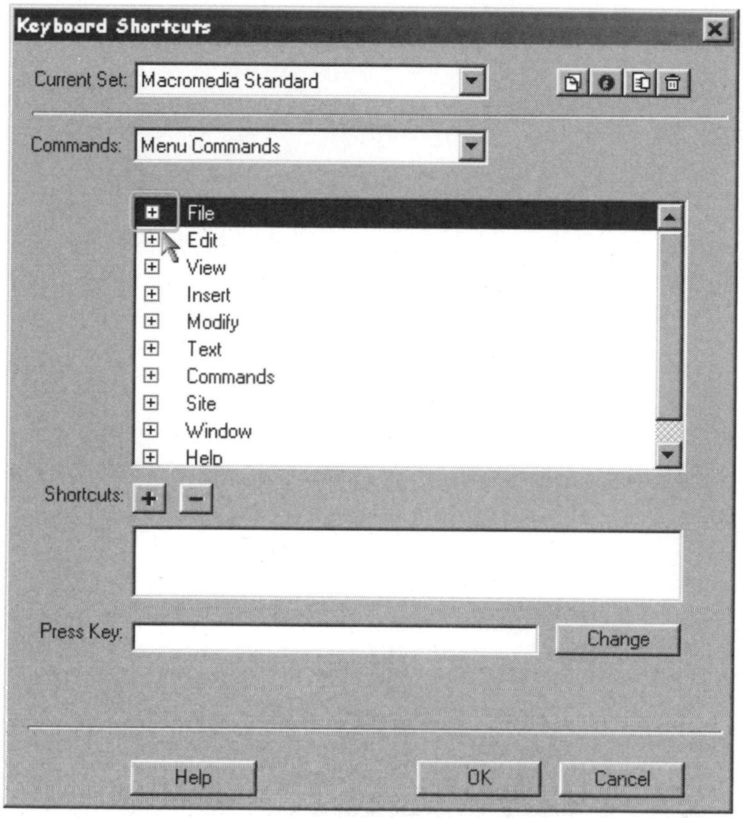

Keyboard Shortcuts

Current Set: Macromedia Standard

Commands: Menu Commands

⊞	File
⊞	Edit
⊞	View
⊞	Insert
⊞	Modify
⊞	Text
⊞	Commands
⊞	Site
⊞	Window
⊞	Help

Shortcuts: + −

Press Key: _____ Change

Help   OK   Cancel

3. Select the specific command you want. Notice that the pre-existing shortcuts attached to that command appear to the right of the command.

4. Press the + button; the cursor moves instantly to the Press Key field.

Keyboard Shortcuts

Current Set: Macromedia Standard

Commands: Menu Commands

File	
New	Ctrl+N
New from Template...	
Open...	Ctrl+O
Open in Frame...	Ctrl+Shift+O
Close	Ctrl+W
Save	Ctrl+S
Save As...	
Save as Template...	
Save All Frames	

Shortcuts: [+] [−]

Press Key: [   ]   Change

Help   OK   Cancel

5. Press the key combination you want to add; the key combination appears in the Press Key field.

6. Click the Change button to assign the new shortcut to the command.

7. Click OK.

Warning

If your key combination is already assigned to another command, Dreamweaver will alert you and let you either reassign the shortcut or simply cancel.

Redefining an Existing Shortcut

If you're not happy with the shortcut for a command, redefining it is quite easy:

1. Go to Edit ➢ Keyboard Shortcuts to open up the Keyboard Shortcuts editor.

2. Click the + next to the command category (File, Edit, View, Insert, etc.) to expand the command you want to work with.

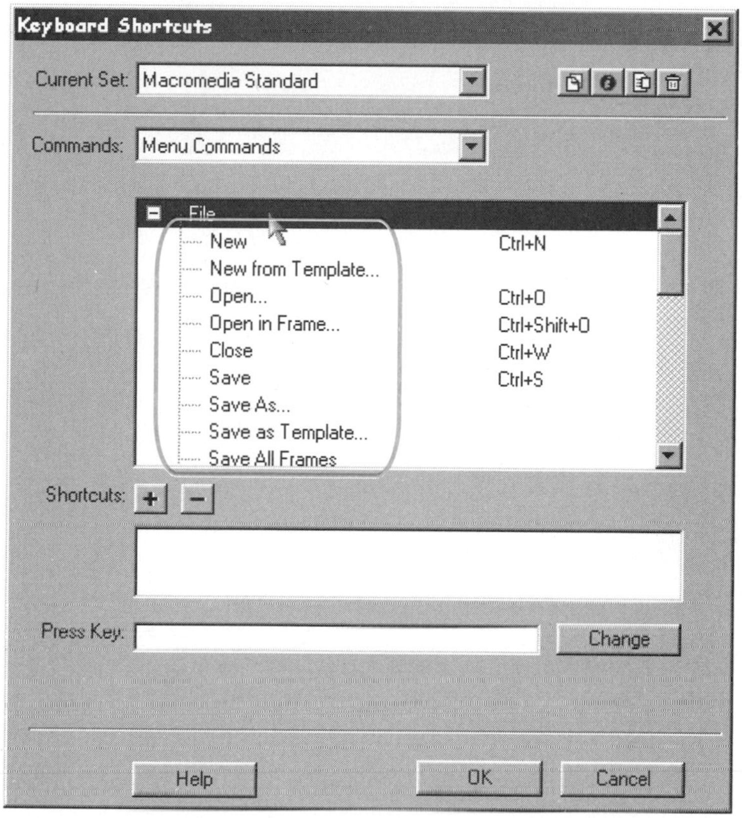

3. Select the specific command you want. Notice that the pre-existing shortcuts attached to that command appear to the right of the command and in the Shortcuts list.

4. Select the shortcut in the Shortcuts list and press the subtract − button. This will remove the current shortcut and pave the way for the addition of a new shortcut.

Keyboard Shortcuts ☒

Current Set: Macromedia Standard ▼   ▣ ⓘ ▣ 🗑

Commands: Menu Commands ▼

⊟ File	
New	Ctrl+N
New from Template...	
Open...	Ctrl+O
Open in Frame...	Ctrl+Shift+O
Close	Ctrl+W
Save	Ctrl+S
Save As...	
Save as Template...	
Save All Frames	

Shortcuts: ＋ －

Ctrl+N

Press Key: [   ]   Change

Help   OK   Cancel

5. Move your cursor to the Press Key field and press the key combination you want to add. The key combination automatically appears in the Press Key field.

6. Click the Change button to assign the new shortcut to the command.

Removing a Shortcut from a Command

Removing a shortcut from a command is almost the same as redefining a shortcut, minus a few steps. To remove a shortcut, follow these steps:

1. Go to Edit ➤Keyboard Shortcuts to open up the Keyboard Shortcuts editor.

2. Click the + to expand the command category (File, Edit, View, Insert, etc.) you want to work with.

Keyboard Shortcuts

Current Set: Macromedia Standard

Commands: Menu Commands

⊟ File	
New	Ctrl+N
New from Template...	
Open...	Ctrl+O
Open in Frame...	Ctrl+Shift+O
Close	Ctrl+W
Save	Ctrl+S
Save As...	
Save as Template...	
Save All Frames	

Shortcuts: + −

Ctrl+O

Press Key: Change

Help   OK   Cancel

3. Select the specific command you want. Notice that the pre-existing shortcuts attached to that command appear to the right of the command and in the Shortcuts list.

4. Select the shortcut in the Shortcuts list and press the − button to remove the current shortcut and pave the way for the addition of a new shortcut.

Keyboard Shortcuts

Current Set: Macromedia Standard

Commands: Menu Commands

⊟ File
- New   Ctrl+N
- New from Template...
- Open...   Ctrl+O
- Open in Frame...   Ctrl+Shift+O
- Close   Ctrl+W
- Save   Ctrl+S
- Save As...
- Save as Template...
- Save All Frames

Shortcuts: + −

Ctrl+O

Press Key: [ ]   Change

Help   OK   Cancel

5. Click the Change button.

6. Click OK.

Defining an External Editor

External editors

Programs that you can launch from within Dreamweaver in order to edit media (such as images, sound, or digital video) or HTML.

One of the neat things about Dreamweaver is that it integrates well with external editors. Whether you're using an image-editing program (like Fireworks or Photoshop) or an HTML text-editing program (like BBEdit or HomeSite), Dreamweaver lets you define a series of editors. These editors allow you to open a given object (an image, for example), edit that object, exit the external editor, and immediately view the changes you've made. For our purposes, we're going to look at how to define an external media editor instead of a text editor. To define a media editor, simply follow these steps:

1. Go to Edit ➤Preferences, or use the shortcut Cmd/Ctrl +U.

2. Select File Types/Editors in the Category list box.

3. In the Extensions list, select the file type for which you want to define an external editor.

4. Click the plus (+) button above the Editors list.

5. When the file navigation screen appears, locate and select the file of the editor you want to associate to the file type.

6. Click OK.

Tip

To make a program your primary editor, simply select it in the Editors list and click the Make Primary button.

Note

In order to launch your external editor, either select the image and go to Edit ➤ Launch External Editor, use the shortcut Cmd/Ctrl+E, or click Edit in the Property Inspector.

Adding Window Size Presets

Earlier in the chapter, you were introduced to the Window Size indicator in the Status Bar of the Document Window and how you can use the drop-down menu to choose from a list of preset Window Sizes. Now you'll learn how you can add your own Window Size presets to the drop-down menu. To do so, follow these steps:

1. Go to Edit ➤ Preferences, or use the shortcut Cmd/Ctrl +U.

2. Select Status Bar in the Category list box.

3. When you click your mouse below the list of preset Window Sizes, a blank edit box will appear. Enter the new width in the Width column.

4. Press Tab and enter the new height in the Height column.

5. Press Tab and enter a description of your custom settings.

6. Click OK.

Changing the Document Size/Download Time Defaults

In addition to being able to change the Window Size, you can also change the speed of the modem that determines the Download Time displayed in the Document Size/Download Time section of the Status Bar. To do this, simply follow these steps:

1. Go to Edit ➢ Preferences, or use the shortcut Cmd/Ctrl +U to open the Preferences Dialog box.

2. Select Status Bar in the Category list box.

Preferences				✕

Category | Status Bar

Category:
- General
- Code Colors
- Code Format
- Code Rewriting
- CSS Styles
- File Types / Editors
- Fonts / Encoding
- Highlighting
- Invisible Elements
- Layers
- Layout View
- Panels
- Preview in Browser
- Quick Tag Editor
- Site
- **Status Bar**

Window Sizes:

Width	Height	Description
600	300	(640 x 480, Max...
760	420	(800 x 600, Max...
795	470	(832 x 624, Max...
955	600	(1024 x 768, M...
544	378	(WebTV)

Connection Speed: 28.8 ▾ Kilobits per Second

Launcher: ☑ Show Launcher in Status Bar

[OK]   [Cancel]   [Help]

3. Just below the Window Size Field, you'll see a drop-down menu labeled Connection Speed (Kilobits per Second). From here you can choose the speed of modem you wish.

Preferences

Category | Status Bar

General
Code Colors
Code Format
Code Rewriting
CSS Styles
File Types / Editors
Fonts / Encoding
Highlighting
Invisible Elements
Layers
Layout View
Panels
Preview in Browser
Quick Tag Editor
Site
Status Bar

Window Sizes:

Width	Height	Description
600	300	(640 x 480, Max...
760	420	(800 x 600, Max...
795	470	(832 x 624, Max...
955	600	(1024 x 768, M...
544	378	(WebTV)

Connection Speed: 28.8 Kilobits per Second

Launcher: 14.4 / 28.8 / 33.6 / 56 / 64 / 128 / 1500 Launcher in Status Bar

OK   Cancel   Help

4. Click OK.

Docking Palettes

One of the new features in Dreamweaver 4 is the ability to dock panels, which means that any panel can be combined with any other panel to create a tabbed floating palette. Ultimately, this makes it considerably easier for you to access tools and information while maximizing your workspace. To dock two palettes, follow these steps:

1. Open any two floating palettes (Assets, Behaviors, Code Inspector, CSS Styles, Frames, History, HTML Styles, Layers, Library, Reference, Templates, or Time-line) by using the Window menu.

2. Click the tab of a palette and drag it over another palette that is open in your workspace.

Note

Because the Object Palette is not a tabbed palette, it is not dockable.

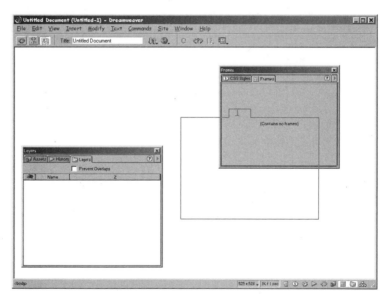

3. When the highlighted black border appears around the target palette, release the mouse button.

Warning

If you click and drag on the title bar instead of the tab of a palette and attempt to drag it to the target palette, there will be no result.

Setting Up a Local Site

Dreamweaver is as much a web site creation and management tool as it is a web page creation tool. Here, web site means a group of linked HTML pages with a shared topic and similar design. While you can create a stand-alone page, Dreamweaver has a host of great tools designed to help you create, manipulate, and manage whole sites. All of these tools revolve around the initial creation of a local site.

The local site (which will include all the files in your site) should reside in a separate folder on your hard drive, mainly because when you get to the point where you want to upload your site to a web server, you'll upload the entire site's folder. By doing this, you ensure that your local site won't be missing any components when you upload it to a remote web server. When you set up your local site, you'll also be able to track and maintain your links.

Warning

If you are inserting elements into a page that sits outside the folder in which your local site resides, Dreamweaver will always prompt you to save them to your local site. If you want your site to be complete when you upload it to your remote server, be sure to take advantage of Dreamweaver's prompt and move external files over to your local site.

Defining Your Site

The first thing you must do when you set up a local site is to tell Dreamweaver where on your hard drive you want your site to reside. You also need to input some additional info about the structure and properties of your local site.

Local site
A group of linked HTML pages with a shared topic and similar design that reside on your computer's hard drive in a specific location.

Setting Local Info

Setting local info entails telling Dreamweaver where your local site will be sitting on your hard drive. To do this, follow these steps:

1. Go to Site ≻ New Site to open the Site Definition dialog box.

2. Make sure Local Info is selected in the Category list box.

3. In the Site Name field, enter the name you want to give to your site.

Site Definition for Unnamed Site 2   ✕

Category   Local Info

Local Info
Remote Info
Design Notes
Site Map Layout
File View Columns

Site Name: Unnamed Site 2

Local Root Folder: C:\E's Media Files\GBL\

☑ Refresh Local File List Automatically

HTTP Address: http://

Entering this address enables the Link Checker to detect HTTP links that refer to your own site.

Cache: ☐ Enable Cache

Enable this option to maintain file and asset information in the site. This speeds up the use of the Asset panel, link management, and Site Map features.

OK   Cancel   Help

Note

The Site Name is not your file name or your page title; it's simply a name that is used when you're working with the Dreamweaver site tools. When you upload your site to a remote web server, the name won't appear anywhere on your pages.

4. Click the browse icon to the right of the Local Root Folder field. When the file navigation screen appears, locate and select the folder on your hard drive where you want your new local site to reside.

5. If you want the structure and content of the site to refresh automatically every time you copy a file into your local site, click the Refresh Local File List Automatically option.

Tip

If you leave the Refresh Local File List Automatically option unchecked, Dreamweaver will copy over files to your local site more quickly.

6. If you know what the URL, or **domain name**, of your site will ultimately be after you've uploaded it to a remote web server, enter it in the HTTP Address field.

Note

If you fill out the HTTP Address field, Dreamweaver can verify links within the site that use absolute URLs. We'll talk more about absolute and relative URLs in Chapter 5, "Working with Hyperlinks."

7. Click OK.

After you've finished entering all the local site info, the Site window will open automatically. On the right side of the window, you'll see your local site. If the section is blank, you need not worry, as your local site just doesn't have any files in it yet.

Setting Web Server Info

Setting your web server info is an important part of setting up a local site. By entering your web site info, you can get access to Dreamweaver's built-in **FTP** tool. Therefore, we're going to take a quick look at how to add web server info to your local site.

1. Go to Site ➢ New Site to open up the Site Definition dialog box.

Site Definition for Unnamed Site 2

Category | Local Info
Local Info
Remote Info
Design Notes
Site Map Layout
File View Columns

Site Name: Unnamed Site 2

Local Root Folder: C:\E's Media Files\GBL\

☐ Refresh Local File List Automatically

HTTP Address: http://

Entering this address enables the Link Checker to detect HTTP links that refer to your own site.

Cache: ☐ Enable Cache

Enable this option to maintain file and asset information in the site. This speeds up the use of the Asset panel, link management, and Site Map features.

OK | Cancel | Help

2. Make sure Remote Info is selected in the Category list box.

Site Definition for Unnamed Site 2

Category
Local Info
Remote Info
Design Notes
Site Map Layout
File View Columns

Remote Info

Access: None

OK   Cancel   Help

3. In the Remote Info field, open the Access drop-down menu and choose either FTP or Local/Network, depending on where your remote server is.

Site Definition for Unnamed Site 2

Category
Local Info
Remote Info
Design Notes
Site Map Layout
File View Columns

Remote Info

Access: None
FTP
Local/Network
None
SourceSafe Database

OK   Cancel   Help

29

4. If you chose FTP, you'll need to fill in access information. This includes the FTP host name (this information can be obtained from either your Internet Service Provider or your Web Hosting Service), the host directory (the exact path of the directory on your FTP host where your web site will reside), and your login and password.

Site Definition for Unnamed Site 2

Category | Remote Info
- Local Info
- Remote Info
- Design Notes
- Site Map Layout
- File View Columns

Access: FTP

FTP Host:

Host Directory:

Login:

Password: ☐ Save

☐ Use Passive FTP

☐ Use Firewall (in Preferences)

Check In/Out: ☐ Enable File Check In and Check Out

[OK] [Cancel] [Help]

Tip

If you want Dreamweaver's FTP tool to remember the password needed to access your FTP host, click the Save check box to the right of the password field. If you don't check the box, you'll need to reenter your password each time you want to access your FTP host.

If you chose Local/Network, you won't have as much information to enter. Simply click the Browse button to the right of Remote Folder field, locate the web server on your local network, and choose the folder where your web site will reside.

5. Click OK.

After you've finished entering all the local site info, the Site window will open automatically. On the right side of the window, you'll see your local site. As before, if the section is blank, you need not worry, as your local site just doesn't have any files in it yet.

Tip

If you don't have direct access to your remote web server, choose FTP. If, for instance, you work at a company that runs its own web server that is attached to a network, choose Local/Network.

Editing an Existing Site

If you've already defined your site but you now want to go back and change some of its information, you're in luck. To edit an existing site, follow these steps:

1. Go to Site ➤ Define Sites to open the Define Sites dialog box.

Tip

You can also access the Define Sites dialog box by selecting Define Sites from the Site drop-down menu in the Site window.

2. Choose from the list the site you want to access, and click Edit.

3. This will open the Site Definition dialog box from which you can make any changes you want.

4. Click OK.

Summary

This chapter explored the program's interface. Further, it introduced you to some ways to customize your working environment. Finally, it covered one of the most important aspects of Dreamweaver: setting up a local site.

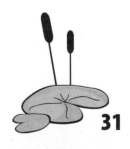

Chapter 2

Setting Up a Dreamweaver Document

Now that you are familiar with the Dreamweaver environment and setting up a local site, there are some things you need to do before adding content to your web page. In Chapter 1, "Starting Up Dreamweaver," you learned how to adjust settings for the entire site. In this chapter, you'll learn how to manage individual documents and set and alter the parameters for an entire page. You'll also learn how to open and save documents, as well as set a target browser and preview your creation.

- Opening and saving documents

- Naming your page

- Changing background color and adding a background image

- Setting text and hyperlink color

- Setting a target browser and previewing your work

Opening a New Document

When launched, Dreamweaver opens a new document by default. However, you may need to start a new Dreamweaver document on your own at some time. To do this, go to File ➢ New, or use the shortcut Command+N (Macintosh) or Ctrl+N (Windows).

You can also create a new document in the Site window by doing the following:

1. Go to Site ➢ Open Site and choose from the list of sites.

2. After the Site window opens, command-click (Macintosh)/right-click (Windows) the folder where you want to create a new file. Choose New File from the menu that opens.

3. Type in the name you want for the new file.

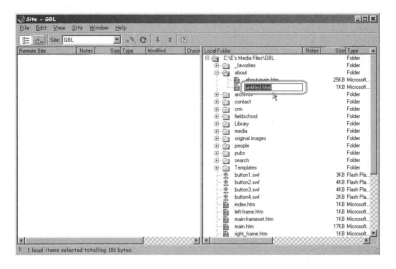

Warning

It's important to remember that when you type in the new name, you make sure it has a suffix of .HTML or .HTM. Otherwise, Dreamweaver won't recognize it as an HTML document.

Opening an Existing Document

After you've worked with Dreamweaver for a while, you are going to start accumulating files that you work with on a regular basis. There are two very simple ways to reopen existing documents. Simply follow these steps:

1. Go to File ➢ Open, or use the shortcut Cmd/Ctrl+O to open the file navigation (Open) screen.

2. Navigate to the area where your file is and select it.

To open an existing file with the Site window, all you need to do is

1. Go to Site ➢ Open Site and choose from the list of sites.

2. Navigate through the folders and double-click the site you want to open.

Warning

Opening an existing document through the Site window won't work if the file you want to open isn't in a defined local site.

Saving a Document

Don't forget to save your documents. To do so, choose File ➢ Save, or use the shortcut Cmd/Ctrl +S.

Warning

If you have multiple documents open and you simply want to save one, make sure you've selected the appropriate document before saving.

Tip

If you have multiple documents open at the same time and want to save them all in one fell swoop, simply choose Save All from the File menu instead of Save.

Setting Your Page Properties

Before you add content in the Document Window, you need to set the page properties in the Page Properties dialog box. When you set the page properties of a given element (text color, for example), you affect all the elements on that page. To open the Page Properties dialog box, do the following:

1. Select Modify ➢ Page Properties from the main program menu bar, or use the shortcut Cmd/Ctrl +J.

2. The Page Properties screen opens.

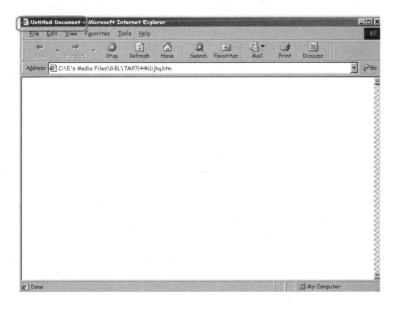

From here we'll look at setting individual page properties with the Page Properties dialog box.

Naming Your Page

Even though it may seem obvious, it's easy to forget to name your page. Naming your page is not the same as naming your file. The name of your page is displayed in the title bar of the browser. Leaving your page untitled will result in an unseemly "Untitled Document" in the title bar of a browser—something that should be avoided at all costs.

To title your page, do the following:

1. Choose Modify ➤ Page Properties, or use the shortcut Cmd/Ctrl +J, to open the Page Properties dialog box.

2. Enter the title of your page in the Title field.

Page Properties

Title: Untitled Document

Background Image: _____ Browse...

Background: ☐ #FFFFFF

Text: ☐ ___ Visited Links: ☐ ___

Links: ☐ ___ Active Links: ☐ ___

Left Margin: ___ Margin Width: ___

Top Margin: ___ Margin Height: ___

Document Encoding: Western (Latin1) ▼ Reload

Tracing Image: _____ Browse...

Image Transparency: ———————| 100%
Transparent   Opaque

Document Folder:
Site Folder: C:\E's Media Files\GBL\

OK / Apply / Cancel / Help

3. Click Apply.

Page Properties

Title: Untitled Document

Background Image: _____ Browse...

Background: ☐ #FFFFFF

Text: ☐ ___ Visited Links: ☐ ___

Links: ☐ ___ Active Links: ☐ ___

Left Margin: ___ Margin Width: ___

Top Margin: ___ Margin Height: ___

Document Encoding: Western (Latin1) ▼ Reload

Tracing Image: _____ Browse...

Image Transparency: ———————| 100%
Transparent   Opaque

Document Folder:
Site Folder: C:\E's Media Files\GBL\

OK / Apply / Cancel / Help

4. Click OK.

Page Properties						

Title: Untitled Document

Background Image: [ ] Browse...

Background: [ ] #FFFFFF

Text: [ ]   *Visited Links:* [ ]

Links: [ ]   *Active Links:* [ ]

Left Margin: [ ]   *Margin Width:* [ ]

Top Margin: [ ]   *Margin Height:* [ ]

Document Encoding: Western (Latin1) [▼]   Reload

Tracing Image: [ ] Browse...

Image Transparency: ———————————— 100%
                      Transparent   Opaque

Document Folder:

Site Folder: C:\E's Media Files\GBL\

[OK] [Apply] [Cancel] [Help]

Tip

You can also title your page by typing in a name in the Page Title field in the toolbar.

Setting a Background Image

You can spice up a web page by adding a background image, which can consist of either one large image or a smaller one that the browser tiles in a continuous pattern. If someone enlarges the browser window, the number of tiles will increase to fill all the available space.

Note

You'll learn more about web graphics in Chapter 4, "Working with Images," but it's important to know that background images are no different than any other kind of web graphic. They must therefore be a GIF, JPEG, or PNG file.

Follow these steps to add a background image to your page:

1. Select Modify ➢ Page Properties, or use the shortcut Cmd/Ctrl +J, to open the Page Properties dialog box.

2. Click the Browse button next to the Background Image field to open the file navigation screen.

3. Navigate to the area where your file is, select it by clicking it once with your mouse button, and click Select. Notice that a small thumbnail preview of the image appears in the Image Preview area when you select an image.

Select Image Source

Look in: media

_notes
1
about_tab
abstracts_title
background
bottom nav bar archives solid

bottom nav bar fs solid
bottom nav bar -opaque
bottom nav bar search solid
bottom nav bar
bottom_nav_bar
bottom_nav-_bar_archives_so

Image Preview

388 x 18 GIF, 3K / 1 sec

File name: bottom nav bar   Select
Files of type: Image Files (*.gif;*.jpg;*.jpeg;*.png)   Cancel

URL: file:///C|/E's Media Files/GBL/media/bottom nav bar.gif
Relative To: Document   Untitled Document
Document should be saved to use this option.   ☑ Preview Images

4. Notice the document's path appears in the Background Image field of the Page Properties dialog box. Click Apply.

Page Properties

Title: Untitled Document   OK

Background Image: file:///C|/E's Media Files/GBL/med   Browse...   Apply

Background: #FFFFFF   Cancel

Text: Visited Links:
Links: Active Links:
Left Margin: Margin Width:
Top Margin: Margin Height:

Document Encoding: Western (Latin1)   Reload

Tracing Image: Browse...

Image Transparency: ──────────┘ 100%   Help
                    Transparent   Opaque

Document Folder:
Site Folder: C:\E's Media Files\GBL\

5. Click OK.

Page Properties dialog box:

- Title: Untitled Document
- Background Image: file:///C|/E's Media Files/GBL/med [Browse...]
- Background: [ ] #FFFFFF
- Text: [ ] Visited Links: [ ]
- Links: [ ] Active Links: [ ]
- Left Margin: [ ] Margin Width: [ ]
- Top Margin: [ ] Margin Height: [ ]
- Document Encoding: Western (Latin1) [Reload]
- Tracing Image: [ ] [Browse...]
- Image Transparency: ————————— 100% Transparent   Opaque
- Document Folder:
- Site Folder: C:\E's Media Files\GBL\

[OK] [Apply] [Cancel] [Help]

Changing Background Color

When you start a new document, the Document Window has a white background. By default, this is the color that Dreamweaver sets as the background color in all new documents. Much like background images, you can easily choose the color you want by using the Color Palette or the Color dialog box.

Web-Safe Colors

Even though most monitors out there can display at least 256 colors (most can display millions), there are really only 216 colors that all computers display exactly the same. These colors are part of what is called the web-safe color palette. These make up the colors that you'll find in the Dreamweaver Color Palette. If you use a color outside the web-safe color palette, the browser will convert it to the closest color it can find in its system palette. As a result, you run the risk of having your colors look slightly different from machine to machine if you stray from the web-safe color palette.

Using the Color Palette

To change the background color of your page with the Color Palette, follow these steps:

1. Choose Modify ➢ Page Properties, or use the shortcut Cmd/Ctrl +J, to open the Page Properties dialog box.

2. Click the swatch (which has the down-pointing arrow in its lower-right corner) next to the Background field to open the Color Palette.

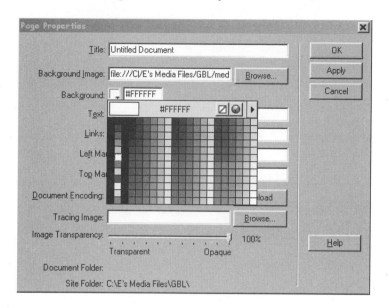

3. Move your mouse over a color you like and click it. Notice that the color swatch in the Page Properties dialog box has changed to the color you've chosen.

4. Click Apply and then OK.

Using the Color Dialog Box

If you aren't satisfied with the colors offered in the Color Palette, you can always use the Color dialog box to choose an alternate color:

1. Go to Modify ➤ Page Properties, or use the shortcut Cmd/Ctrl +J, to open the Page Properties dialog box.

2. Click the swatch next to the Background field to open the Color Palette.

3. Move your mouse over the open Color dialog box icon in the top-right corner of the Color Palette and click it.

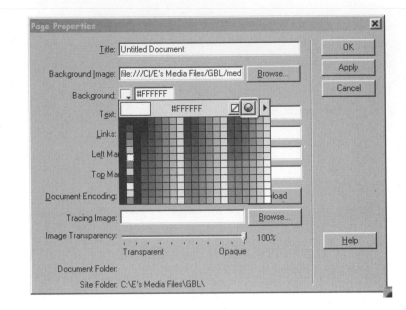

4. Next, you'll see a screen like this:

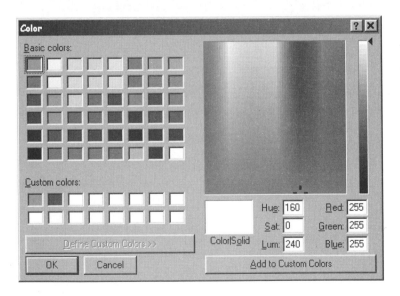

5. From here, you can choose the specific color you want by entering its corresponding numerical **RGB** code.

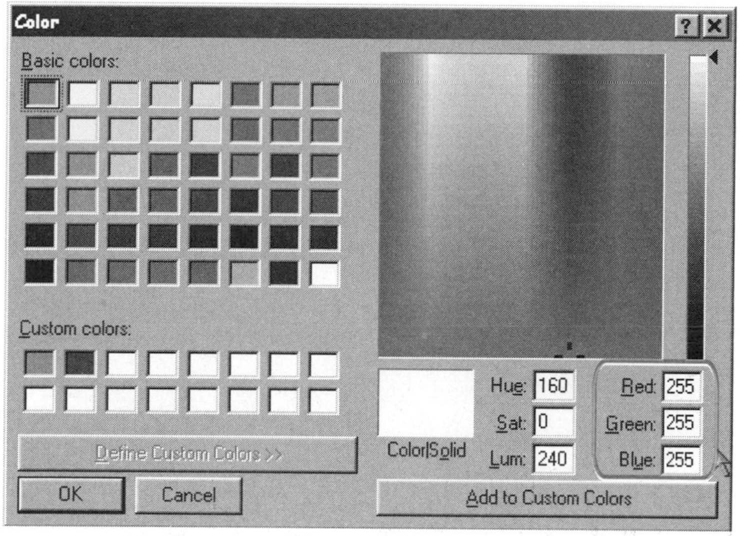

Or you can choose one by clicking the **hue** selector.

RGB

Stands for the colors **R**ed-**G**reen-**B**lue. In web design (and design for computer monitors), colors are defined by the combination of these three colors.

Hue

The actual color of an object. Hue is measured as a location on a color wheel, expressed in degrees. Hue is also understood as the names of specific colors (blue, red, yellow, etc.).

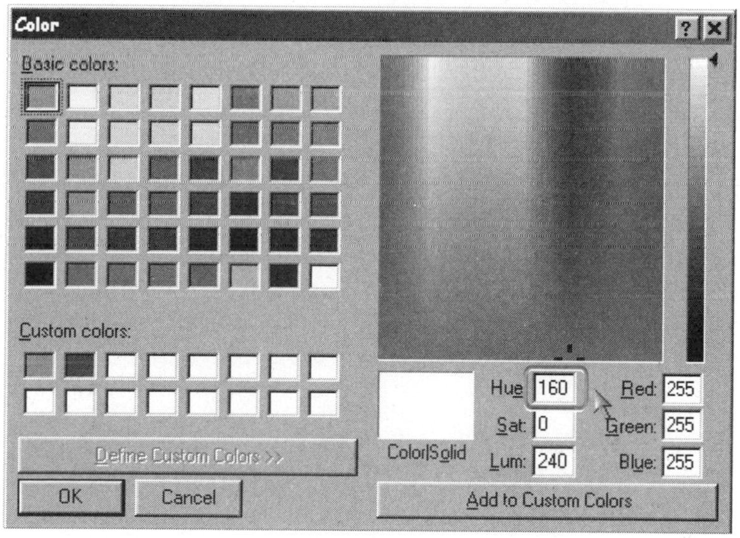

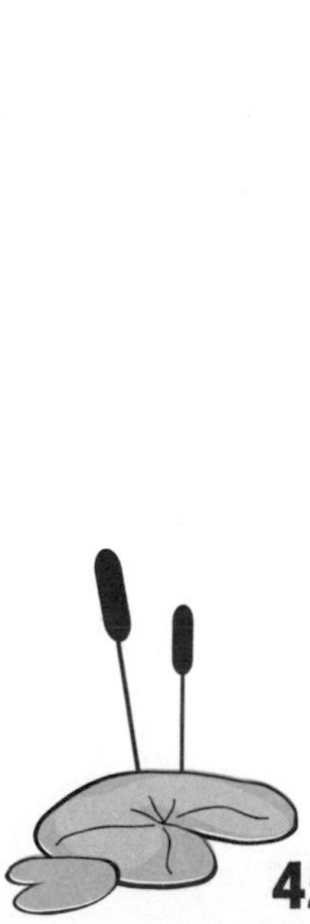

Or you can set the shade with the shade slider.

Tip

If you decide to use the Color dialog box to choose a color that isn't in the Color Palette—and plan on using the color in other projects—make sure you write down the RGB code. It's great to find the perfect color but a shame to forget it!

Changing Text Color

Changing the color of your page's text is similar to changing your page's background color:

1. Go to Modify ➢ Page Properties, or use the shortcut Cmd/Ctrl +J, to open the Page Properties dialog box.

2. Click the swatch next to the Text field.

Page Properties ☒

Title: Untitled Document

Background Image: _____ Browse...

Background: ☐ #FFFFFF

Text: ☐ ____ Visited Links: ☐ ____

Links: ☐ ____ Active Links: ☐ ____

Left Margin: ____ Margin Width: ____

Top Margin: ____ Margin Height: ____

Document Encoding: Western (Latin1) ▾ Reload

Tracing Image: _____ Browse...

Image Transparency: ▬▬▬▬▬▬▬⌐ 100%
Transparent   Opaque

OK
Apply
Cancel

Help

Document Folder:

Site Folder: C:\E's Media Files\GBL\

3. The Color Palette will open, allowing you to immediately choose the color you wish or to open and select from the Color dialog box.

4. Click Apply and then OK.

Changing Link Color

Changing your text color involves only one color, but changing your hyperlink color involves three different colors: link color, visited link color, and active link color. The process is exactly the same if you're changing the regular link color, the active link color, or the visited link color.

Tip

When you set the link color, you are choosing the color that the link normally appears when someone first comes to your page.

Visited link

A hyperlink that has changed color (the default is purple) to indicate that that the user has already visited that web page.

Active link

The state of a hyperlink as it is being clicked. The default color for an active link is red.

To change the link color (or active link/visited link color) for your page, follow these steps:

1. Go to Modify ➢ Page Properties, or use the shortcut Cmd/Ctrl +J, to open the Page Properties dialog box.

2. Click the swatch next to the Links field (or the Active Links/Visited Links field).

Page Properties		✕

Title: Untitled Document — OK

Background Image: _____ Browse... Apply

Background: ▢ Cancel

Text: ▢   Visited Links: ▢

Links: ▢   Active Links: ▢

Left Margin: ▢   Margin Width: ▢

Top Margin: ▢   Margin Height: ▢

Document Encoding: Western (Latin1) ▾ Reload

Tracing Image: _____ Browse...

Image Transparency: ▮————————— 100%   Help

Transparent   Opaque

Document Folder:

Site Folder: C:\E's Media Files\GBL\

3. This will open the Color Palette and allow you to choose the color you wish or to open and select from the Color dialog box.

4. Click Apply and then OK.

Tip

For the most part, the classic blue (which is the default color) underlined text is universally recognized as a link. If you change your link color to something else, there is the possibility that people might not even recognize it as a link. So, unless there is some pressing design need to change the link color (or you detest the color blue) stick with the default.

Working with a Tracing Image

Remember when you were a kid, you used tracing paper to trace images from a book or magazine so that you could get your picture just right? Macromedia has brought all of this back with the Tracing Image feature.

Most web design is conceived and fleshed out on paper before it goes near a screen. The problem with this is that something on paper doesn't always translate to digital form

exactly as the designer imagined. This is where tracing images come in. Essentially, you can scan a pen and paper design and add it to the background of your web page.

Tip

A tracing image isn't the same thing as a background image. When you go live with your page (or simply preview it in a browser), the tracing image isn't seen. The only time it's ever visible is when you are working on your creation in the Document Window.

Follow these steps to try it:

1. Select Modify ➢ Page Properties, or use the shortcut Cmd/Ctrl +J, to open the Page Properties dialog box.

2. Click the Browse button to the right of the Tracing Image field.

3. Navigate to the appropriate file and select it. Notice that a small thumbnail preview of the image appears in the Image Preview area of the file navigation screen.

4. Click Apply.

5. You can adjust the transparency of the tracing image by using the slider.

Page Properties	
Title: Untitled Document	OK
Background Image: [ ] Browse...	Apply
Background: [ ]	Cancel
Text: [ ] Visited Links: [ ]	
Links: [ ] Active Links: [ ]	
Left Margin: [ ] Margin Width: [ ]	
Top Margin: [ ] Margin Height: [ ]	
Document Encoding: Western (Latin1) Reload	
Tracing Image: file:///C|/E's Media Files/GBL/med Browse...	
Image Transparency: [———————|] 100% Help	
Transparent Opaque	
Document Folder:	
Site Folder: C:\E's Media Files\GBL\	

Previewing Your Work in a Browser

Early Browsers

After **Mosaic** was released, the size of the World Wide Web increased exponentially. Many companies soon realized that the browser was the key to the whole shebang, and they quickly responded. The most notable were Microsoft and Netscape. Despite the fact that both companies have become the giants of the scene, many smaller companies are offering their own take on the browser.

You can never be absolutely sure what kind of browser is being used to view your page, and most browsers display HTML a little differently. This is where Dreamweaver's Preview in Browser function comes in. You can set it so that a simple stroke of a hotkey will load your page in a browser of your choice.

Warning

You can preview work only in a browser that you have installed on your computer.

Mosaic
The first true web browser. Developed by the National Center for Supercomputing Applications (NCSA) at the University if Illinois. Mosaic was primarily distinguished by the fact that it was able to display graphics.

Hotkey
A single key, usually defined by the user, that launches a particular program or function of a program.

51

Adding a Target Browser

Before you can preview your work in a browser, you first need to tell Dreamweaver which browsers you've loaded on your computer and which hotkeys you want to associate with them. To set a target browser, follow these steps:

1. Choose Edit ➢ Preferences from the main program menu bar, or use the shortcut Cmd/Ctrl +U, to open the Preferences dialog box.

2. Select Preview in Browser from the Category list box.

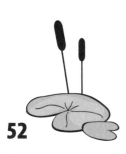

3. Click the plus (+) symbol to open the Add Browser dialog box.

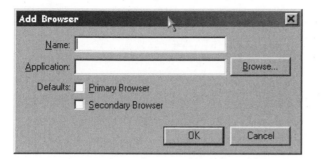

4. In the Name field, type in the browser name as you want it to appear in the browser list.

5. Click Browse to open the file navigation screen. Navigate to the browser program file and select it.

6. Click OK.

Tip

Depending on your preference, you can designate two browsers as primary and secondary. By doing this, you are designating the default, which is the primary browser.

Editing Your Browser List

You may find it necessary to edit your browser list. Follow these steps to do so:

1. Go to Edit ➢ Preferences, or use the shortcut Cmd/Ctrl +U, to open the Preferences dialog box.

2. Select Preview in Browser from the Category list box.

3. Select the browser to edit and click the Edit button to open the Edit Browser dialog box.

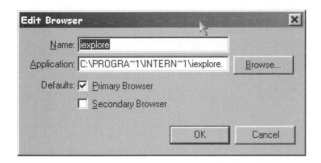

4. Make your changes and then click OK.

Launching Your Target Browser

Once you've defined your target browser and its associated hotkeys, there are two ways to preview your creation:

1. Hit the hotkey you defined for the target browser. In most cases, the default for your primary browser is F12 while the default for your secondary browser is Cmd/Ctrl +F12.

2. Click the Preview in Browser button in the Toolbar to open a drop-down list of target browsers to choose from.

Tip

If you've only defined one target browser in the Preferences dialog box, clicking the toolbar's Preview in Browser button will automatically launch that browser.

Summary

This chapter covered opening and saving documents and setting page properties such as background color, page title, and text color. Most importantly, this chapter emphasized previewing your work in a browser.

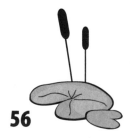

Part 2

Creating Content in Dreamweaver

Now that you can set up your Dreamweaver document, you can now learn how to add basic content. In the next couple of chapters, you'll learn the foundations of a good web site. You'll start by adding and manipulating text, then move on to adding and working with images.

Creating Content in Dreamweaver

Chapter 3

Adding and Manipulating Text

Despite the fact that the World Wide Web is becoming an increasingly visual medium, the majority of information on it is still textual. In this chapter, you're going to learn how to add and edit text in Dreamweaver. You're also going to learn how you can organize blocks of text on your page. Topics include the following:

- ◆ Creating and placing text
- ◆ Changing text size
- ◆ Changing text font and color
- ◆ Aligning, indenting, and outdenting text
- ◆ Adding Horizontal Rules
- ◆ Creating text lists
- ◆ Adding special characters

Creating and Placing Text

There really is no mystery to creating and placing text in Dreamweaver. Just click your cursor in the Document Window and type. It's just that easy! The real fun comes when you get to change the text from its default size, font, and color into something that will fit with the design of your page. While this process is pretty painless, there are some important issues when it comes to text and the web.

Tip

You can also copy text from another application, switch to Dreamweaver, click the cursor at your chosen insertion point in the Document Window, and choose Edit ➤ Paste as Text. Dreamweaver won't preserve text formatting from the other application, but it will preserve line breaks.

Note

The **default** font for text in Dreamweaver is Times/Times New Roman, while the default color is black and default size is 3.

Default
A preset option that will always be followed unless the user enters a command to the contrary.

Text, Typeface, and Fonts

When you work with text, you'll find that the words **text**, **font**, and **typeface** are often used in much the same way. Don't be fooled, however; there is a big difference between them. Text refers generally to any characters that combine to make up a written document of some sort (whether a word, a sentence, or this book). A font, on the other hand, is a complete set of characters in a particular size and style. This includes the letters, the numbers, and all of the special character you get by pressing the Shift, Option, or Command (Macintosh) or Ctrl (Windows) keys. Finally, a typeface contains a series of fonts. For example, the typeface Arial contains the fonts Arial, Arial Bold, Arial Italic, and Arial Bold Italic.

Manipulating Text

Manipulating text you've created in Dreamweaver is relatively straightforward and, for the most part, happens with either the Property Inspector or the Text menu. Changing the text size, font, color, and style are the most common changes.

Sizing Text

Web text size is not represented in the same way that digital text normally is. Instead of being measured by point size, web text size is represented on a sizing scale from 1 to 7:1 being the smallest size and 7 being the largest size. Dreamweaver offers two sizing systems: absolute and relative. While separate, they are both based on the 1–7 sizing system, which can be pretty limiting.

Tip

There are ways around the limitations of web text sizing. The most popular is to create an image of text. If you do this, you can make the text in your image any size and insert it into your document. Dreamweaver sees it simply as an image, not text. You can also create non-standard text using the Flash Text feature new to Dreamweaver 4.

Setting Absolute Text Size

There are 7 sizes in the absolute sizing system—size 1 is the smallest, and size 7 is the largest. Each size is fixed and is one increment larger than the previous. To change the absolute size of text, follow these steps:

1. Select the text whose size you want to change.

2. If you don't already have the Property Inspector open, go to Window ➢ Properties, or use the shortcut Cmd/Ctrl+F3.

3. Click the Size drop-down menu in the Property Inspector. You'll notice that there are three sets of numbers: −1 to −7, +1 to +7, and 1 to 7. Choose from the 1 to 7 list (these are the absolute sizes).

4. When you select a size from the Size drop-down menu, the text will automatically change to reflect your choices.

Note

As you work your way through this book, you'll find that there are often two ways to do the same procedure. For the most part, the first involves using the Property Inspector, while the other involves using Dreamweaver's menu. To help you make a choice that is best for you, both will be discussed.

You can also change the absolute size of text using the Text menu. To do this, follow these steps:

1. Select the text whose size you want to change.

2. Go to Text ➢ Size and choose the size you want.

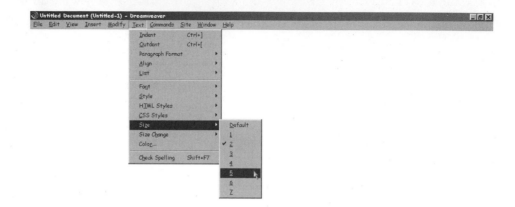

Setting Relative Text Size

Unlike the absolute sizing system, relative sizing doesn't really have a fixed size. When you choose a relative size, you increase or decrease the current text size by a number of fixed increments. Follow these steps to set relative text size:

1. Select the text whose size you want to change.

2. If you don't already have the Property Inspector open, go to Window ➢ Properties, or use the shortcut Cmd/Ctrl+F3.

3. Click the Size drop-down menu in the Property Inspector. There are three sets of numbers: −1 to −7, +1 to +7, and 1 to 7. Choose from either the +1 to +7 list or the −1 to −7 list (these are the relative sizes).

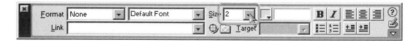

If you choose from the minus (−) sizes, you will decrease the absolute size of the text by the increment you've chosen (if you choose −3, the absolute size of the text will be decreased 3 increments). The same applies for the plus (+) sizes that increase the absolute size of the text.

Warning

You can't use the relative sizes to increase text size more than 7 or decrease text size lower than 1.

You can also change the relative size of text using the Text menu. Simply select the text whose size you want to change, go to Text ➢ Size Change, and make your size choice.

Changing Fonts

One of the great things about fonts is that there are so many out there that you can always find one to suit your needs. The good news is that you aren't limited to one font on the web. The bad news is that, for all intents and purposes, you are limited to three: Times New Roman, Courier New, and Arial for Windows; and Times, Courier, and Helvetica on the Mac. But there is actually quite a bit you can do with only four fonts.

Why Only Four Fonts?

Web browsers can only display fonts that are installed on the user's system. If a font that is used on a web page isn't installed on the user's computer, the browser substitutes a font that **is** installed. This can cause trouble when the web designer used a specific font, but the web browser displays the page in a totally different font. However, this can be easily avoided.

Every personal computer in the English-speaking parts of the world that was built in at least the last eight years was shipped with what are called **system fonts**. These fonts consist of Times New Roman, Courier New, and Arial (on the PC), and Times, Courier, and Helvetica (on the Mac). If you design with these fonts, you don't have to worry about having them substituted, because everyone has them.

Note

Through the efforts of Microsoft and Apple, the fonts Verdana and Georgia are shipped with most desktop computers these days. As a result, you can add them both to the list of fonts you can design with.

System fonts
The basic fonts that a computer's operating system uses to display system type.

You can change fonts in Dreamweaver by doing the following:

1. Select the text whose font you want to change.

2. If you don't already have the Property Inspector open, go to Window ➢ Properties, or use the shortcut Cmd/Ctrl+F3.

3. Choose the new font from the Font drop-down menu in the Property Inspector.

Try changing text fonts using the Text menu. Just select the text whose font you want to change, select Text ➢ Font, and make your choice.

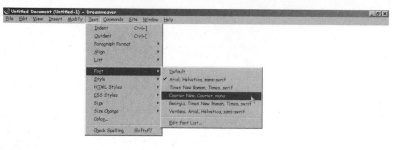

Warning

You've probably noticed the Edit Font List option in both the Text ➢ Font menu and the font list drop-down menu in the Property Inspector. By clicking this, you can add or subtract fonts to the list that is displayed. Unless you've got some solid design reasons, because of the issues I mentioned above, I strongly suggest that you leave the Edit Font List alone...in order to avoid the temptation.

Changing Font Color

When it comes to font color, you've got to take into consideration the color issues we discussed in the last chapter. Beyond those limitations, you've got a really nice palette of colors that you can apply to text. In Dreamweaver, changing font color is pretty easy:

1. Select the text whose color you want to change.

2. If you don't already have the Property Inspector open, go to Window ➢ Properties, or use the shortcut Cmd/Ctrl+F3.

3. Click the swatch to open the Color Palette.

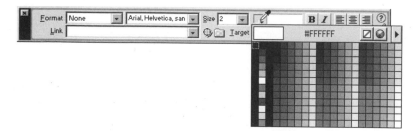

4. Move your mouse over a color you like and click it. Notice that the color of your text automatically changes.

Tip

If you want to choose a color that isn't contained in the Color Palette, follow the procedure described in the "Using the Color Dialog Box" section of the previous chapter.

To change text color by using the Text menu, select the text whose color you want to change, go to Text ➤ Color to open the Color Dialog box, and make your choice.

Tip

Unless there is a really strong design reason, try to avoid using "hyperlink blue" for your fonts. Because that color has become so synonymous with a link, users might actually mistake your text for a link and get frustrated when they click it and there's no result.

Changing Text Styles

One of the other neat things you can do with text is change its style by using **bold**, *italic*, underline, and others. As with many of Dreamweaver's features, there are two ways to change text style. The first way, which limits the amount of styles you can actually apply to text, uses the Property Inspector:

1. Select the text whose style you want to change.

2. If you don't already have the Property Inspector open, go to Window ➤ Properties, or use the shortcut Cmd/Ctrl+F3.

3. Click either the Bold or the Italic button in the top-right corner of the Property Inspector.

4. Here, I've added bold and italic to some text.

You can make text both **bold** and *italicized*. You can also use ***both styles*** at the same time.

To get a much wider range of possible text styles, you can use the Text menu. Just select the text and choose a style from the Text ➤ Style drop-down menu.

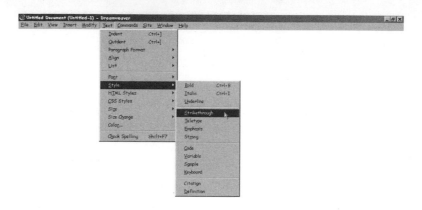

Tip

It's a good idea to play around with all available styles so that you can get a general idea of how each looks with different text sizes and fonts.

Organizing and Laying Out Text

Because HTML isn't a design medium, the control you have over how your text is laid out on your page is somewhat limited. You can control how your text is aligned to the page and some very limited text block separation and arrangement techniques. However, once you've had a little practice with the available options, you'll come up with some good designs.

Aligning Text

The most basic way you can lay out text is with the Alignment tool, with which you can justify text to the left, to the center, and to the right. Like most things in Dreamweaver, there are two ways to align text: the Property Inspector or the Text menu. To do the first of these, just follow these steps:

1. Place the cursor anywhere in the line of text you want to justify.

2. If you don't already have the Property Inspector open, go to Window ➤ Properties, or use the shortcut Cmd/Ctrl+F3.

3. Click one of the three Align buttons in the top right-hand corner of the Property Inspector.

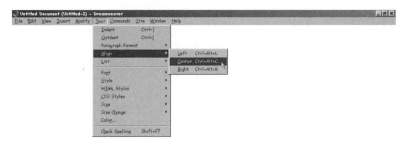

You can also align text with the Text menu. Just place the cursor anywhere in the line of text you want to justify and make your alignment selection from the Text ➤ Align drop-down menu.

Tip

To align text, you can also use the shortcuts Cmd/Ctrl+Option/Alt+L (left), Cmd/CtrlOption/Alt+C (center), or Cmd/Ctrl+Option/Alt+R (right).

Inserting a Horizontal Rule

Up until now, all the things we've discussed have involved making an alteration to existing text. A Horizontal Rule, a great tool for breaking up blocks of text, is really an object that needs to be inserted into a document. Essentially, a Horizontal Rule is a straight line that extends across the Document Window. To insert a Horizontal Rule, follow these steps:

1. Place the cursor where you'd like to insert the Horizontal Rule.

2. If you don't already have the Object Palette open, go to Window ➤ Objects, or use the shortcut Cmd/Ctrl+F2.

3. Click the Insert Horizontal Rule button.

Changing Horizontal Rule Dimensions

After you've inserted a Horizontal Rule, there are a few changes you can make to its appearance. First, you can change its dimensions:

1. Select the Horizontal Rule.

2. If you don't already have the Property Inspector open, go to Window ➢ Properties, or use the shortcut Cmd/Ctrl+F3.

3. Type a value into the Width or Height field. If you want the Horizontal Rule to always occupy a certain width of the page (regardless of how large or small the Document Window is), choose the percent sign (%) from the drop-down menu to the right of the Width (W) field. If you want its width to remain fixed, choose pixels.

Changing Horizontal Rule Alignment

To change the alignment of the Horizontal Rule, simply do the following:

1. Select the Horizontal Rule you want to edit.

2. If you don't already have the Property Inspector open, go to Window ➤ Properties, or use the shortcut Cmd/Ctrl+F3.

3. Choose Left, Center, or Right from the Align drop-down menu in the top right of the Property Inspector.

Warning

If the width of your Horizontal Rule occupies your entire Document Window, changing its alignment will have no effect.

Shading the Horizontal Rule

You can also decide whether you want your Horizontal Rule to be shaded or not. When it's shaded, it has a three-dimensional look. If it isn't shaded, the Horizontal Rule looks like a simple solid bar.

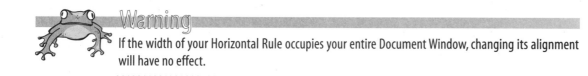

To change this, follow these steps:

1. Select the Horizontal Rule you want to edit.

2. If you don't already have the Property Inspector open, go to Window ➤ Properties, or use the shortcut Cmd/Ctrl+F3.

3. Either select or unselect the Shading button (depending on whether you want your Horizontal Rule shaded or unshaded, respectively).

Indenting and Outdenting Text

As in the case of a word processor, you might find the need to indent portions of your text. When you indent text in Dreamweaver, the line automatically wraps to accommodate the changes. As a result, the section of text that you indent will occupy more vertical space. To indent blocks of text with the Property Inspector, follow these steps:

1. Select the text that you want to indent, or place your cursor somewhere on the line you are indenting.

2. If you don't already have the Property Inspector open, go to Window ➤ Properties, or use the shortcut Cmd/Ctrl +F3.

3. Click the Text Indent button in the bottom-right corner of the Property Inspector to indent one increment.

Try indenting with the Text menu. Simply select the text you want to indent and go to Text ➤ Indent or use the shortcut Cmd/Ctrl+] (right bracket).

Note

The opposite of indenting is outdenting. If you want to outdent text, you either click the Text Outdent button in the Property Inspector or go to Text ➤ Outdent. If text is already flush with the left edge of the Document Window, using the Outdent feature won't change anything.

Formatting Text with Lists

In Dreamweaver, you can format text into lists. Lists are a good way to organize information. Dreamweaver provides two primary list types: ordered and unordered.

Creating an Ordered List

An **ordered list**, which is often referred to as a numbered list, presents information in a sequential, structured manner. To create an ordered list, you need to do the following:

1. Place the cursor where you want the ordered list to begin.

2. If you don't already have the Property Inspector open, go to Window ➤ Properties, or use the shortcut Cmd/Ctrl+F3.

Ordered list
A list in which each item is prefaced by a sequentially ordered number or letter.

3. Click the Ordered List button in the bottom-right portion of the Property Inspector. You'll notice that the number "1" automatically appears.

4. Type the first item in your list.

5. Hit Enter. You'll notice that the next number in the list automatically appears on the next line.

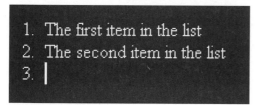

1. The first item in the list
2. The second item in the list
3. |

6. Repeat steps 4 and 5 until you've completed the list.

7. To terminate the list, hit Enter twice.

Inserting an ordered list with the Text menu is just as easy. All you need to do is place the cursor where you want the ordered list to begin and go to Text ➢ List ➢ Ordered List. Then follow steps 4 through 7 above.

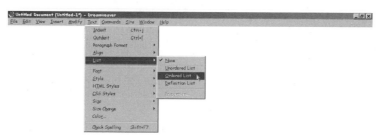

Creating an Unordered List

Unlike an ordered list where the items are organized in a systematic manner, an unordered list—also referred to as a bulleted list—is designed to present information that doesn't need to be in any specific sequence. To create an ordered list, follow these steps:

1. Place the cursor where you want the unordered list to begin.

2. If you don't already have the Property Inspector open, go to Window ➢ Properties, or use the shortcut Cmd/Ctrl+F3.

Unordered list
A list in which each item is prefaced by a symbol (usually a bullet) and is not sequentially ordered.

3. Click the Unordered List button that is in the bottom-right portion of the Property Inspector. You'll notice that a bullet automatically appears.

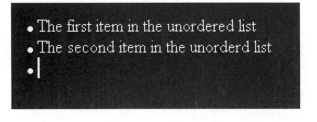

4. Type the first item in your list.

5. Hit Enter. You'll notice that another bullet automatically appears on the next line.

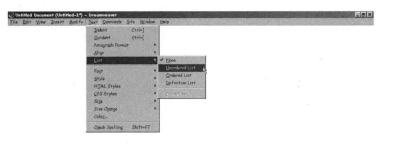

- The first item in the unordered list
- The second item in the unorderd list
-

6. Repeat steps 4 and 5 until you've completed the list.

7. To terminate the list, simply hit Enter twice.

You can also insert an unordered list by using the Text menu. All you need to do is place the cursor where you want the unordered list to begin and select Text ➢ List ➢ Unordered List. Then follow steps 4 to 7 that were described above.

Tip

You can change the default look of either the bullets or numbers with the List Properties dialog box. Simply select a list you've already made, click the List Item button in the bottom-right corner of the Property Inspector (you must expand the Property Inspector to use it) to open up the List Properties dialog box, and make your changes.

Inserting Special Characters

What happens if you need to insert a character that doesn't appear on your keyboard? You might come across a situation where you need to insert a pound sterling symbol (£), a copyright symbol (©), or a trademark symbol (™), for example. You can add many special characters with the simple click of the mouse:

1. Place the cursor where you want to insert the special character.

2. If you don't already have the Object Palette open, go to Window ➢ Objects, or use the shortcut Cmd/Ctrl+F2.

3. Click the down-pointing arrow in the top-right corner of the Object Palette and choose Characters from the drop-down list.

Tip

If you want to insert a character that isn't in the Characters panel of the Object Palette or on the Insert menu, either choose Insert Other Character in the Characters panel or choose Other from the Insert ➢ Characters menu to choose from a larger set of special characters.

4. Click the character you want to insert into your document.

You can also insert a special character into your document by using the Insert menu. Place the cursor where you want to insert the special character and select Insert ➢ Characters. From there you can choose the specific special character you want to insert.

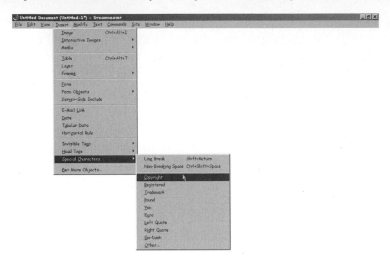

Checking your Spelling

Spelling errors are a surefire way to send people away from your site. Dreamweaver has made checking a document for spelling errors very easy by including a spell-check feature.

To use the spell check feature, select Text ➢ Check Spelling, or use the shortcut Shift+F7. Any errors will be picked up and changed in the Check Spelling dialog box.

Using Flash Text

One of the coolest technologies to come down the pipe in recent years is Flash, Macromedia's vector animation program. Since objects in Flash are **vector graphics**, they look considerably smoother and crisper than graphics normally seen on the web.

In Dreamweaver 4, Macromedia has given you the ability to create editable vector text with the new Flash Text feature. By using the Flash Text feature, you can avoid the font and size limitations that we covered at the beginning of this chapter. In addition, if you use Flash vectors instead of an image for text, your graphics are scalable, smaller in file size, and they look good when they're printed.

Vector graphics

A type of graphic in which the position of the pixels are mathematically calculated. Because of this, vector graphics consistently scale smoothly.

Warning

It's important to note that users will still need to have the Flash plug-in installed on their computers to be able to view any Flash text inserted into documents.

To use the Flash Text tool, just follow these steps:

1. Place your cursor where you want to insert the Flash text.

2. If you don't already have the Object Palette open, go to Window ➤ Objects, or use the shortcut Cmd/Ctrl+F2.

3. Click the Insert Flash Text button in the Common panel to open the Insert Flash Text dialog box.

You can also access the Insert Flash Text dialog box by going to Insert ➢ Interactive Images ➢ Flash Text.

4. Choose a font from the Font drop-down menu in the top-left corner of the Flash Text dialog box. The menu will include all the fonts you presently have loaded on your system.

5. Enter the font size in the Size field. Unlike with normal web text, you can use points for Flash text.

6. Click the color swatch to open the Color Palette. From here you can choose the color you want your Flash text to be.

7. Type your text in the Text Field.

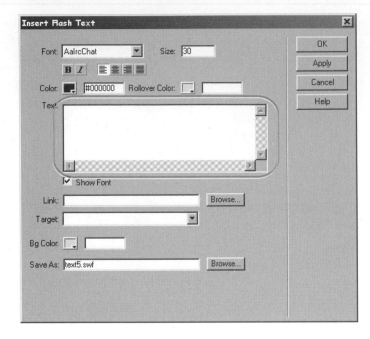

8. Enter a filename in the Save As field. You can use the default filename (`text1.swf` and so on), but you must enter something in this field. The file is automatically saved to the same directory as the current document.

9. Click Apply and then OK. Here is an example of what your text might look like:

Flash Text at its greatest!

Note

By setting the other properties in the Flash Text dialog box (such as rollover color, link, and target), you can change your Flash text into an interactive button that links to another portion of your site.

Summary

This chapter covered all things textual in Dreamweaver. It looked at how you add text to the Document Window and then how you can manipulate the text (resize, align, etc.). It also discussed why you should limit your designs to the system fonts. While the reasons for this may seem unimportant at this stage of the game, they will definitely come into play down the road. The chapter described ways you can arrange your text by using indents and outdents, ordered and unordered lists, and Horizontal Rules. It also looked at the Flash Text tool, which is new to Dreamweaver 4.

Chapter 4

Working with Images

We use images in many interesting ways to cover all sorts of online information, and Dreamweaver makes adding images to your web page a painless process. As in the case of web type in the last chapter, there are some issues that you need to be aware of when dealing with web images. This chapter will begin by looking at some of these issues and then go on to inserting and manipulating images with Dreamweaver.

- ◆ Understanding web image formats

- ◆ Placing images in a document

- ◆ Manipulating images

Plug-ins

A software extension that provides added capabilities to the browser, for purposes such as viewing, hearing, or saving specially formatted files.

GIF

Stands for Graphics Interchange Format. GIF images are the most widely used graphic format on the web. GIF images display up to 256 colors.

Interlaced

Storing partial data from a single graphic image in sequence. The purpose of interlacing is to have a partial image initially appear on-screen rather waiting for the entire image to load before it's viewable.

JPEG

Stands for Joint Photographic Experts Group. JPEGs contain millions of colors and are usually best suited for complex photorealistic images.

PNG

Stands for Portable Network Graphic. Developed originally by Macromedia, PNGs support indexed color (256 colors), grayscale, true-color images (millions of colors), and transparency.

Understanding Web Image Formats

One of the first and most important things you need to know about web image formats is that, without the help of plug-ins, the web supports only three types of images: GIFs, JPEGs, and PNGs. Before we dive into how Dreamweaver deals with images, it's a good idea to become familiar with the strengths and weaknesses of each of the three image formats.

GIF

GIF stands for Graphics Interchange Format. Developed originally by CompuServe in the late '80s, GIFs are the workhorse image of the web. Because the format itself can display a maximum of only 256 colors, GIFs are best used for relatively simple images with flat colors and are generally smaller in size (in terms of kilobytes). One of the great things about GIFs is that they come in a few different forms: transparent GIFs, interlaced GIFs, and animated GIFs. Transparent GIFs allow the background upon which they are placed to be visible. When they are created, the user decides which color should be transparent in the image. Interlaced GIFs are structured in such a way that they come into focus slowly as the browser loads the image. Animated GIFs are simply a series of images saved in the same file. When a browser loads this file, all the images in the file are displayed in sequence, creating an animation much like a digital flip book.

JPEG

JPEG stands for Joint Photographic Experts Group. JPEGs came along sometime after GIFs and were designed specifically to display photographic or continuous color images. Their main strength comes from the fact that they can display millions of colors. As a result, JPEGs tend to have larger file sizes than GIFs. Actually, as the quality of the JPEG increases, so does its file size. Unfortunately, JPEGs come in only one "flavor": no transparency, no interlacing, and definitely no animation.

PNG

PNG stands for Portable Network Graphic. Developed originally by Macromedia, PNGs are less straightforward than GIFs or JPEGs. They were designed to combine the best of both GIFs and JPEGs; they can therefore support indexed color (256 colors), grayscale, true-color images (millions of colors), and transparency. The problem with PNGs is that they have spotty browser support. Microsoft Internet Explorer (4.0 and later) and Netscape Navigator (4.04 and later) only partially support the display of PNG images. Because PNG is the native file type of Fireworks, Dreamweaver has some fairly sophisticated tools that are geared specifically toward PNG manipulation and management.

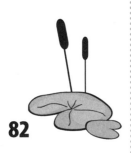

Warning

For Dreamweaver to recognize a PNG, the file must have the .png extension.

Placing Images

Now that you know the basic web image types, you can insert an image into the Document Window. To do so, follow these steps:

1. Place the cursor where you want to insert the image.

2. If you don't already have the Object Palette open, go to Window ➢ Objects, or use the shortcut Command+F2 (Macintosh) or Ctrl+F2 (Windows).

3. Click the Insert Image button in the Common panel of the Object Palette.

4. When the file navigation screen appears, locate the image you want to insert and select it.

To place an image using the Insert menu, follow these steps:

1. Place the cursor where you want to insert the image.

2. Go to Insert ➢ Image, or use the shortcut Command+Option+I (Mac) or Ctrl+Alt+I (Win).

3. When the file navigation screen appears, locate the image you want to insert and select it.

Manipulating Images

Here you'll learn some of the basics of manipulating your image to fit into the overall design of your page. As with similar processes in Dreamweaver, the majority of image manipulation is done with the Property Inspector.

Because HTML isn't a design medium, you are going to be fairly limited in what you can do with images. However, given a firm grounding in what you can do, you'll be able to come up with many interesting creations.

Justifying an Image

One of the most basic things you can do with an image after it's been inserted into a Dreamweaver document is to justify it to the page. Because an image can't be moved around a document as it can in an image-editing program like Fireworks or Photoshop, aligning it becomes an important part of your final design. Aligning an image is almost the same as aligning text:

1. Place your cursor anywhere along the line that contains the image.

2. If you don't already have the Property Inspector open, go to Window ➢ Properties, or use the shortcut Cmd/Ctrl+F3.

3. Click one of the three alignment buttons in the top-right corner of the Property Inspector.

Aligning an Image with Text

Now that you can justify images to the page, let's explore how to align images with text. It's a fair bet that when you create a web page, you're going to have more than just text or just images. You will ultimately want to combine the two in a pleasing visual form.

If you've already experimented with images and text in the same document, you've probably noticed that they don't integrate very well. In fact, images have the tendency to break up the flow of text.

You can, however, exert some control over how the text on your page interacts with an image. Follow these steps to align an image to text:

1. For the purposes of this exercise, insert an image somewhere in a block of text.

2. Select the image you want to align by clicking it with your mouse.

3. If you don't already have the Property Inspector open, go to Window ➢ Properties, or use the shortcut Cmd/Ctrl+F3.

4. Go to the Align drop-down menu in the upper-right corner of the Property Inspector.

Choose Top from the drop-down menu. You'll notice that only one line aligns itself with the top of the image. (We'll cover the other options in the next section.)

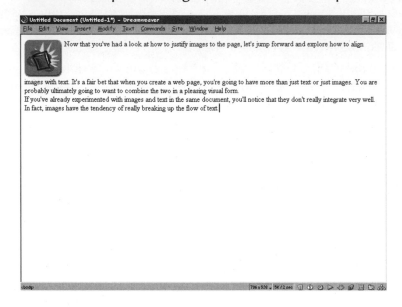

Exploring Alignment Options

The Align drop-down menu has many more choices than just Top. Each aligns text to an image in a different way.

Text Top   If you choose Text Top, the top line of the text aligns with the top of the image.

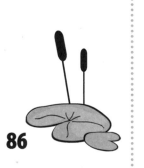

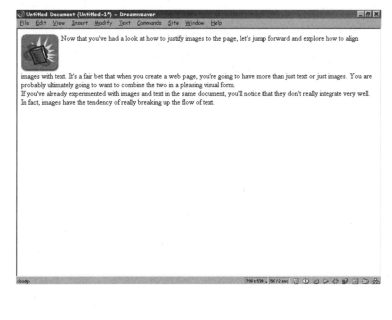

Note

While it may appear that Text Top is the same as Top, there are some differences. Basically, Top aligns text with the highest item on the line, and Text Top aligns the tallest character in the line with the top of the image.

Bottom and Baseline   These choices align the baseline of the first line of text to the bottom of the image.

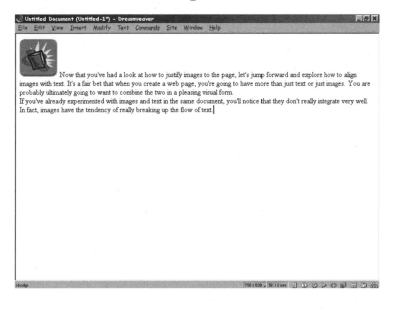

Absolute Bottom   This aligns the bottom of the image to the absolute bottom of the lowest characters (which includes descenders, as in the letter "g" or "j").

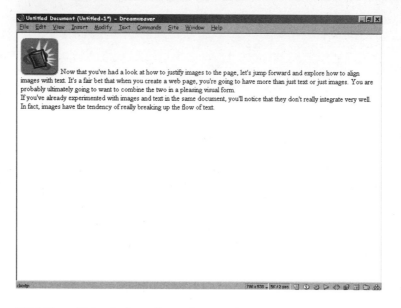

Middle   This choice aligns the text baseline with the middle of the selected object.

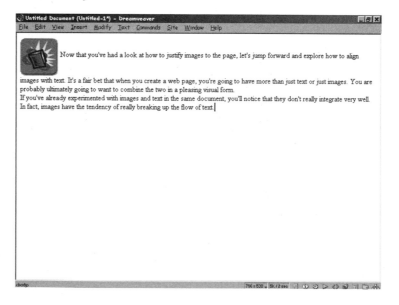

Absolute Middle   This choice aligns to the absolute middle of the current line.

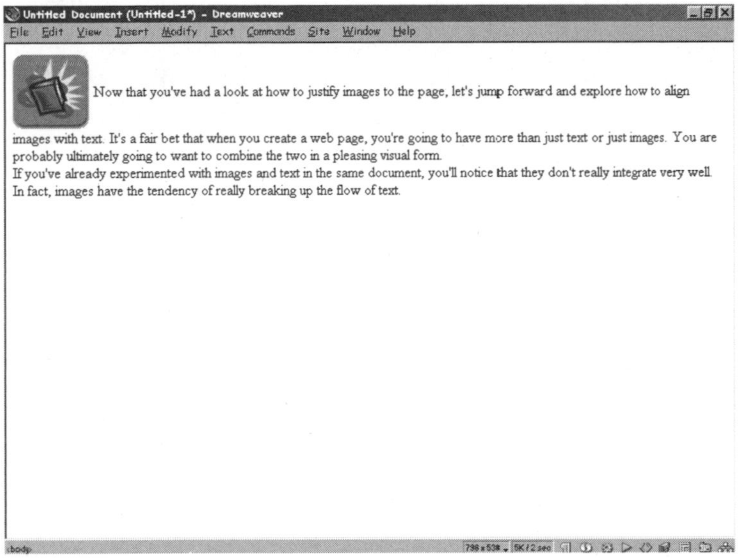

Left   This places the image on the left margin and wraps the text around it to the right. If left-aligned text comes before the image on the line, it forces left-aligned objects to wrap to a new line.

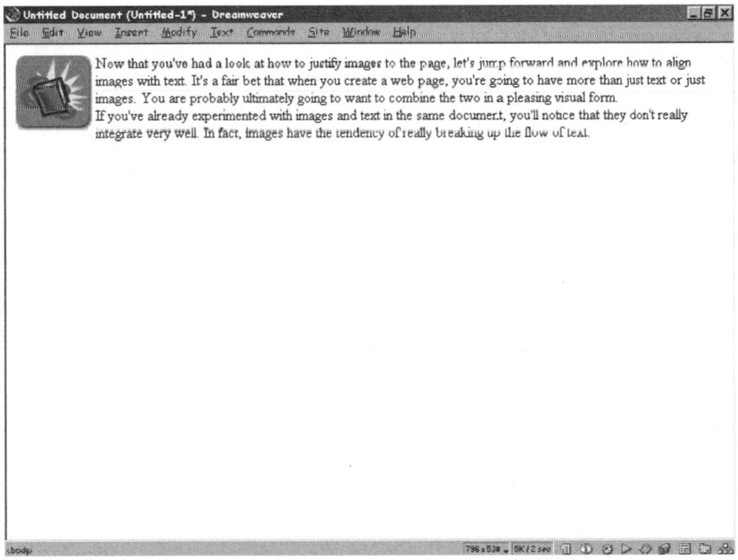

Right   This places the image on the right margin and wraps the text around it to the left. If right-aligned text precedes the image on the line, it will force right-aligned objects to wrap to a new line.

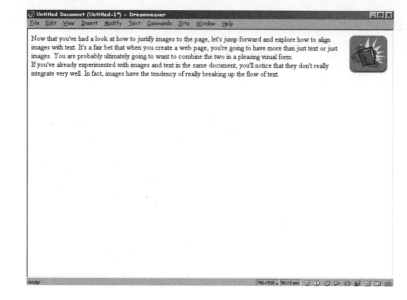

Note

While the differences between standard alignment and an absolute alignment are sometimes difficult to detect, they do indeed exist. Basically, an absolute alignment will use the entire height of a line of text (which is determined by the very top of the highest character and the very bottom of the lowest character) for alignment purposes.

Note

Browser default generally means a baseline alignment. However, the default may differ depending on the browser that is being used to view the page.

Resizing an Image

Resizing an image in Dreamweaver is really quite easy, but there are some important things you need to know before you start. Images in Dreamweaver are of very low quality (72 dpi to be exact). If you increase their size, you'll see a marked loss in quality. The images will appear grainy and pixilated.

Note

Making an image smaller in Dreamweaver won't cause the same problems as making it larger.

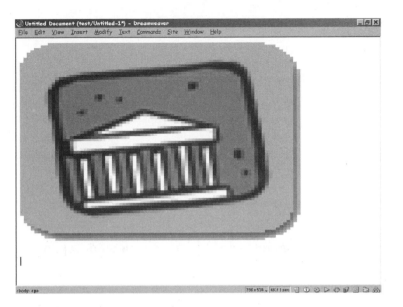

Resizing images in a Dreamweaver document creates the same stretched effect as if you were to draw a picture on a balloon and then blow it up. Unless you have some pressing design need, avoid changing the size of an image in Dreamweaver. Instead, make sure the image is the exact size you want it to be before you insert it into a Dreamweaver document.

Resizing an Image with the Property Inspector

When you resize an image, you aren't resizing the original file, but the way it looks in your Document Window. To resize an image you've inserted into your Dreamweaver document, follow these steps:

1. Select the image you want to resize by clicking it with your mouse.

2. If you don't already have the Property Inspector open, go to Window ➢ Properties, or use the shortcut Cmd/Ctrl +F3.

3. Enter a new width and height in the W and H boxes in the Property Inspector. Remember that all dimensions are in pixels, as opposed to another unit of measure like centimeters or millimeters.

4. The dimensions of the image will automatically update when you either hit Enter or move the cursor out of either of the fields.

Resizing an Image with the Resize Handles

You can also resize an image by using the resize handles:

1. Click the image you want to resize.

2. Click and hold one of the resize handles.

3. Drag the resize handles until your image is the desired size and release your mouse button.

Note

If you have the Property Inspector open while you are using the resize handles, you'll notice that the values in the W and H boxes will change dynamically to reflect the increasing size of the image.

Tip

If you hold down Shift while dragging the resize handles, your image will maintain the same proportions.

Reverting to the Original Image Size

If you've increased the size of an image and aren't happy with the result—and you've forgotten its original dimensions—there is an easy way to revert back to the original size of the document. To do so, follow these steps:

1. Select the image you've resized by clicking it with your mouse.

2. If you don't already have the Property Inspector open, go to Window ➢ Properties, or use the shortcut Cmd/Ctrl +F3.

3. Click the Reset Size button in the lower-right corner of the expanded Property Inspector.

Using the ALT Tag

The ALT tag is probably one of the most overlooked features you can use in creating an image. Essentially, the ALT tag (ALT is short for alternative) is designed to provide extra information about an image when the image isn't visible. This handy feature provides information for text-only browsers (browsers that can't display images) or for browsers that are set to download images manually.

The ALT tag will pop up (similar to a Tool Tip) when the user moves their mouse over an image.

This is what an ALT tag looks like when it pops up in a browser.

Also, the ALT tag provides a way for a screen-reading program to "speak" to the blind or visually-impaired user. Without the ALT tag, screen readers are incapable of giving any audible feedback on the image itself. To add an ALT tag to your image, follow these steps:

1. Select the image you want to add the ALT tag to.

2. If you don't already have the Property Inspector open, go to Window ➤ Properties, or use the shortcut Cmd/Ctrl +F3.

3. Enter your desired text in the ALT field of the Property Inspector.

Setting a Low Source Image

A Low Source image is a helpful feature if you're designing a site that you know will be viewed by people with slower Internet connections. With this feature, you're essentially designating an image to load before the main image. Many designers use a small black-and-white version of the main image because it loads more quickly than the main image and gives visitors an idea of what they're waiting to see.

Warning

The Low Source image must have the same dimensions as the regular image it is associated with.

Let's add a Low Source image:

1. Click the main image for which you want to set the Low Source image.

2. If you don't already have the Property Inspector open, go to Window ➢ Properties, or use the shortcut Cmd/Ctrl+F3.

3. Click the Browse button to the right of the Low Src field in the expanded Property Inspector.

Image, 3K	W 83	Src mages/monkey_icon.gif	Align Browser Default
	H 83	Link	Alt This is what an ALT tag l
Map	V Space	Target	Border
	H Space	Low Src	Edit / Reset Size

4. When the file navigation screen opens, locate the file you want to set as the Low Source image and select it.

Adding a Border to an Image

During the creative process, you may need to add a solid border around an image; for instance, you may want to set off an image from the surrounding material on the web page. To add a border to an image in Dreamweaver, follow these steps:

1. Select the image you want to add a border to.

2. If you don't already have the Property Inspector open, go to Window ➢ Properties, or use the shortcut Cmd/Ctrl+F3.

3. Enter a value (width in pixels) in the Border field of the expanded Property Inspector.

Warning

Use image borders sparingly, as overuse can result in a very unattractive design.

Launching an External Image Editor

In Chapter 1, "Starting Up Dreamweaver," you learned how to define your external media editors. Now comes the time when you can put all that work into practice:

1. Select the image you want to launch in the external editor by clicking it with your mouse.

2. If you don't already have the Property Inspector open, go to Window ➤ Properties, or use the shortcut Cmd/Ctrl +F3.

3. Expand the Property Inspector (if it isn't already) by clicking the down-pointing arrow in the bottom-right corner of the Inspector.

4. Click the Edit button in the bottom-right portion of the Property Inspector to launch the external editor associated with the particular image type.

5. Once you've made changes to the image in the external editor, save it and exit. The image in Dreamweaver will be automatically updated to reflect the changes.

Note

After saving the changes in the external image editor, Dreamweaver might prompt you to update the page. Say Yes if you want your image to be updated!

Summary

This chapter looked at how to insert images into your Dreamweaver documents and then what can be done to them after they've been inserted. It covered such topics as aligning an image to the page, aligning an image to text, resizing an image, adding an ALT tag, adding image borders, and using an external image editor. Beyond the mechanics of adding and manipulating images in Dreamweaver, the chapter looked at the three web image formats: GIFs, JPEGs, and PNGs. If you're interested in learning more about the various web image formats, check out some of Webmonkey's informative articles (`http://hotwired.lycos.com/webmonkey/design/graphics/`).

Part 3

Dreamweaver Site-Building Skills

Now that you've learned some of the fundamentals of creating a web site in Dreamweaver, you'll learn to use some site-building skills you'll need to bring your digital creation to fruition. You'll start by working with hyperlinks, and then move on to working with tables, one of the most powerful layout tools available.

Dreamweaver
Site-Building Skills

Chapter 5

Working with Hyperlinks

After setting up a local site on your hard drive, you're going to want to create links between documents and other types of media. This is where hyperlinks come in. Hyperlinks are really the core of HTML. They allow the user to move effortlessly between documents, whether they're on the same server or another server entirely. Dreamweaver allows you to create links between HTML documents, multimedia files, images, and downloadable files. In this chapter, you'll learn how to add hyperlinks to both images and text and how to manage some of the finer points of link manipulation. This chapter includes the following topics:

- Understanding hyperlinks
- Adding hyperlinks to text and images
- Changing link color
- Creating a named anchor
- Setting a link target
- Creating an Image Map
- Creating an e-mail link

Understanding Hyperlinks

Before we start looking at how you add links in Dreamweaver, there are some general issues you need to know. In Dreamweaver, you'll be working with two types of links: relative and absolute. They really aren't two different types of links, technically, but two different ways of representing the same thing.

Using Absolute Links

Absolute links

A link that includes the entire URL (the `http://` protocol, the domain name, and the filename).

An absolute link—or path—provides a complete URL. For example, `http://www.macromedia.com/dreamweaver` is an absolute URL. It's important to include the `http://` protocol at the beginning of absolute URLs. The general rule is that absolute links are used to link to a document that sits on another server. You can certainly use absolute links for documents on the same server, but it's much easier if you use relative links instead.

URL

URL, which stands for **U**niform **R**esource **L**ocator, is an address referring to an HTML document on the Internet.

Using Relative Links

Relative links

A type of shorthand link that is used to refer to a file on the same server.

Relative links are a little less straightforward than absolute links. These links are a cross between an instruction and shorthand. The link itself contains information that uses the current folder on the server as a reference point for finding the linked document. These instructions are called the path. A relative link doesn't need the same sort of structure and protocol (`http://`) that an absolute link does. As a result, relative links can be used only to refer to documents that are on the same server. If you are a little confused right now, don't worry too much. When you are using relative URLs, Dreamweaver does all the work for you.

Note

For more information on relative URLs, see Mastering Dreamweaver 4 and Fireworks 4 by David Crowder and Rhonda Crowder (Sybex, 2001).

Adding Hyperlinks

In this section, you'll learn how to add links to both images and text. You'll also take a look at the handy Point to File utility that will make the creation of links a snap. In addition, you'll learn how to create a named anchor, a great feature that allows you to create a link to another point on the same page, and how to set up a link target.

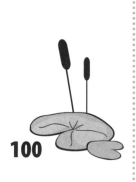

Note

To change the color of links (including visited and active links), refer to Chapter 2, "Setting Up a Dreamweaver Document."

Adding a Relative Link to Text

Dreamweaver automatically takes care of the technical coding details necessary when creating a relative hyperlink.

To add a relative link to text, follow these steps:

1. Select the text that you want to turn into a link.

2. If you don't already have the Property Inspector open, go to Window ➢ Properties, or use the shortcut Command+F3 (Macintosh) or Ctrl+F3 (Windows).

3. Click the browse icon to the right of the Link field.

4. When the file navigation screen appears, locate and select the file to which you want to link. You'll notice that the relative link, complete with the necessary path, has appeared in the Link field.

5. To activate the link, either hit Enter or click off of the Property Inspector anywhere in the Document Window.

Adding an Absolute Link to Text

To add an absolute link, follow these steps:

1. Select the text that you want to turn into a link.

2. If you don't already have the Property Inspector open, go to Window ➢ Properties, or use the shortcut Cmd/Ctrl+F3.

3. In the Link field, type in the full URL of the document you're linking to.

4. To activate the link, either hit Enter or click your mouse anywhere outside of the Property Inspector in the Document Window.

> **Tip**
>
> Sometimes the full absolute URL is long and easily forgotten. Here's a tip: Open the file in a browser, and then copy and paste the full URL into the Link field of the Property Inspector.

Using the Point to File Icon

The Point to File icon is a handy tool that works in tandem with the Site window to provide a visual way to link to files within your site. Be forewarned, however, that despite its usefulness, using the Point to File icon can be a little frustrating. But let's give it a try:

1. Select the text that you want to turn into a link.

2. If you don't already have the Property Inspector open, go to Window ➢ Properties, or use the shortcut Cmd/Ctrl+F3.

3. If you don't already have a local site opened in the Site window, go to Site ➢ Open Site and select the site you are currently working on.

4. Align the top of the Property Inspector with the bottom of the Site window. You'll find that the Property Inspector will actually snap into place next to the Site window.

> **Tip**
>
> If the Site window disappears, use your toolbar to maximize the Site window (which brings it back into view).

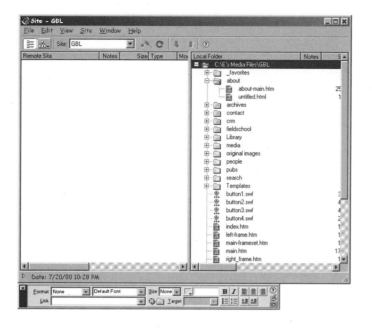

5. Click the Point to File icon, hold your mouse button down, and drag the mouse to the file in the Site window that you want to create a link to.

6. Release your mouse button over the desired file. The relative URL automatically appears in the Link field.

103

Creating a Named Anchor

At one time or another, you have probably experienced an extremely long web page that uses links to transport you to specific locations in the text. This is done with named anchors (sometimes called jump links), which create an anchor that you can link to from within a page. You can also use them to jump to a specific location in another page entirely. Follow these steps to insert a named anchor:

1. Place the cursor where you want to insert the named anchor.

2. Go to Insert ➢ Invisible Tags ➢ Named Anchor, or use the shortcut Cmd+Option+A (Mac) or Ctrl+Alt+A (Win). (Alternatively, you can click the Named Anchor button in the Invisibles panel of the Object Palette.)

3. Type a name in the Anchor Name field of the Insert Named Anchor dialog box.

4. Click OK.

Tip

Unfortunately, Dreamweaver doesn't keep track of the names you give to the named anchor, so it's a good idea to keep the name simple and descriptive and to write it down so you don't forget it.

5. If an anchor marker doesn't appear at the insertion point, go to View ➢ Visual Aids and select Invisible Elements.

Linking to a Named Anchor on the Same Page

To create a link to the named anchor, do the following:

1. Select either the text or image you want to link to the named anchor.

2. If you don't already have the Property Inspector open, go to Window ➢ Properties, or use the shortcut Cmd/Ctrl+F3.

3. In the Link field of the Property Inspector, type # followed by the name of the anchor you've just created.

4. Either hit Enter or click your mouse anywhere off of the Property Inspector in the Document Window. The text that you linked to the named anchor has now been activated.

Linking to a Named Anchor on a Different Page

You can take the process one step further and create a named anchor on another page to which you can link. The steps are almost the same as linking to a named anchor, but they take place over two different pages instead of one:

1. Place the cursor where you want to insert the named anchor.

2. Go to Insert ➢ Invisible Tags ➢ Named Anchor, or use the shortcut Cmd+Opt+A (Macintosh) or Ctrl+Alt+A (Windows). (Alternatively, you can click the Named Anchor button in the Invisibles Panel of the Object Palette.)

3. Type a name in the Anchor Name field of the Insert Named Anchor dialog box.

Insert Named Anchor	✕
Anchor Name:	OK
typenameoftheanchorhere	Cancel
	Help

4. Click OK.

5. Open (or create) a page into which you want to insert the link to the named anchor you created in the previous step (this means that you'll have two separate Document Windows open at the same time—in one, you've just inserted the named anchor, and in the other you'll create the link).

6. Call the first page, the one in which you inserted the anchor, anchor.html. Call the second page, the one that has the actual link, link.html.

7. In `link.html`, select either the text or image you want to link to the named anchor. (In the example below, an image has been selected.)

8. If you don't already have the Property Inspector open, go to Window ➢ Properties or use the shortcut Cmd/Ctrl+F3.

9. Click the browse icon to the right of the Link field in the Property Inspector.

10. When the file navigation screen appears, locate the file in which you placed the anchor (in our case, `anchor.html`) and select it.

   The correct filename and path appear in the Link field.

11. Directly after the filename and path, type # followed by the name of the anchor you inserted in the first document (in our case, `anchor.html`).

12. To activate the link, either hit Enter or click your mouse in the Document Window anywhere off of the Property Inspector.

Blank target

When a blank target is set for a link, the file will load up into a new browser window.

Self target

When a self target is set for a link, the file will load up in the same browser window and replace the previous page.

Warning

For the named anchor to work properly, make sure that there aren't any spaces between the path/filename and the beginning of the # and link name.

Setting a Link Target

By setting a link target, you are telling the browser to upload the file either in a totally new window over the previous window (this is called a blank target) or in the same window (which is called a self target).

Note

The default link target for most browsers is "self," so if you leave the link target alone, your link will upload in the same browser window.

Here you will set a link target for a relative link. (The process is exactly the same for absolute links.) You'll also focus on setting a blank link target, as Dreamweaver will automatically set a self-link target by default if one isn't specified.

1. Select either the text or image that you want to turn into a link.

2. If you don't already have the Property Inspector open, go to Window ➢ Properties, or use the shortcut Cmd/Ctrl+F3.

3. Click the browse icon to the right of the Link field.

4. When the file navigation screen appears, locate and select the file to which you want to link. The relative link and the necessary path appear in the Link field.

5. Click the down-pointing arrow to the right of the Target field in the Property Inspector to open the Target drop-down menu.

6. Choose _blank from the drop-down menu.

7. To activate the link, either hit Enter or click off of the Property Inspector anywhere in the Document Window.

Note

While link targets are used extensively in frames, further coverage goes beyond the scope of this book. For more information, see Mastering Dreamweaver X and Fireworks X by David Crowder and Rhonda Crowder (Sybex, 2001).

Creating E-Mail Links and Image Maps

So far you've learned the basics of creating and manipulating links in Dreamweaver. Now you'll learn some of the more interesting link-oriented features of Dreamweaver, such as creating an e-mail link and an Image Map, which is a fusion of images and links.

Creating an E-Mail Link

An e-mail link is a link that opens a blank message window in the e-mail program of the user's browser. When the blank message window appears, it contains the e-mail that was included in the link. To insert an e-mail link, follow these steps:

1. Click your cursor where you'd like to insert the e-mail link in the Document Window.

2. Go to Insert ➢ E-Mail Link.

3. In the Insert E-Mail Link dialog box, enter the text of the link in the Text field.

4. In the E-Mail field, enter the appropriate e-mail address.

5. Click OK.

You can also add an e-mail link manually by using the Property Inspector.

1. Select either the text or image that you want to turn into a link.

2. If you don't already have the Property Inspector open, go to Window ➢ Properties, or use the shortcut Cmd/Ctrl+F3.

3. In the Link field of the Property Inspector, type **mailto:** followed by the appropriate e-mail.

4. To activate the link, either hit Enter or click your cursor off of the Property Inspector anywhere in the Document Window.

Warning

In order for the e-mail link to work properly, make sure that there aren't any spaces in the text you manually enter in the Link field.

Creating an Image Map

An Image Map is a fusion of a link and an image. You've probably noticed that when you add a link to an image, the entire image becomes a link. With an Image Map, you can designate portions of an image (using hotspots) as links. You can even have multiple hotspots in the same image, each linking to a different page. Creating an Image Map involves two different processes: inserting the image and defining hotspots and links.

Image Map

An image in which certain areas, defined by hotspots, act as links to different files.

Tip

Before you start inserting hotspots and defining links, you should have a really good idea to which areas of your image you want to attach links.

Inserting the Image

1. If you haven't already inserted the image you want to map, do so first by following the procedure outlined in Chapter 4, "Working with Images."

2. Select the image you want to map.

3. If you don't already have the Property Inspector open, go to Window ➢ Properties, or use the shortcut Cmd/Ctrl+F3.

4. If the Property Inspector is not expanded, click the expander button in the lower-right corner.

5. In the lower-left corner of the expanded Property Inspector, you'll see the Image Map tools.

6. In the Map field, enter a unique name for your Image Map.

7. Now you can go ahead and define your hotspots.

Defining Hotspots

Depending on the general shape of the area that you want to turn into a hotspot, you have three tools to choose from: Rectangular Hotspot, Circular Hotspot, and Polygon Hotspot. The Circular Hotspot and Rectangular Hotspot are self-explanatory. The Polygon Hotspot, on the other hand, is designed to create an irregular area that is neither a circle nor a rectangle.

To define the hotspot area, do one of the following (depending on the shape of the hotspot you want):

◇ Click the Rectangular Hotspot button, move the crosshair (+) over the place in the image where you want the hotspot, and click and drag until you've covered the area you want. Release the mouse button when you're finished.

◇ Select the Circular Hotspot button, move the crosshair over the place in the image where you want the hotspot, and click and drag until you've covered the area you want. Release the mouse button when you're finished.

◇ Select the Polygon Hotspot button, place the crosshair along any edge of the irregular area, and click your mouse once. You'll notice that a light blue point appears where you click your mouse. Move the crosshair to the next point along the edge of the irregular area and click your mouse button again. You'll notice that a line appears between the two points. Continue clicking, adding points along the edge of the irregular area until it's fully outlined (and shaded) with the hotspot.

Once you've successfully defined a hotspot, the Hotspot view of the Property Inspector will appear.

Then do the following:

1. Click the browse icon to the right of the Link field.

2. When the file navigation screen appears, locate and select the file that should open when the hotspot is clicked. If this file is not in your local site, type the absolute link in the Link field.

3. Choose a link target by clicking the down-pointing arrow to the right of the Target field.

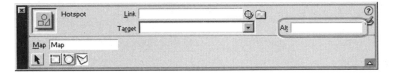

4. Enter any alternate text that you want associated with the hotspot in the Alt field.

5. To activate the Image Map, click your mouse anywhere off of the Property Inspector in the Document Window.

Tip

Once you've created the Image Map, you can edit it by clicking the hotspot you want to edit (which is represented by the pale blue area on the image) and then making any changes. To move a hotspot around, simple click and drag it.

Summary

This chapter looked at hyperlinks. It discussed the differences between absolute and relative links. It also talked about adding links to both text and images. It explored how you can add links to specific sections on the same page (or on another page) by using named anchors. The chapter closed with a look at link targets, e-mail links, and Image Maps.

Chapter 6

Working with Tables

The placement of images, text, and other elements, and their relation to one another, contribute to the layout of your page. Until now, you haven't had a lot of control over where elements were placed in your page, because you've been restricted by the inherent limitations of HTML. But that's going to change drastically with tables–probably the most powerful layout tools in Dreamweaver. Dreamweaver offers two different creative environments in which you can create tables. The first is the Standard view, whose tools have been around since the first version of Dreamweaver. The second, Layout view, is a revolutionary new feature in Dreamweaver 4 that allows you a great deal more control over the creation and manipulation of tables. Topics in this chapter include the following:

- Understanding tables
- Creating tables in Standard view
- Manipulating Standard view tables
- Adding content to a cell
- Working with cells, rows, and columns
- Creating tables and cells in Layout view
- Manipulating tables and cells in Layout view

Understanding Tables

As with tables in word processing or spreadsheet programs, web-based tables are composed of rows, columns, and cells. Content, whether visual or textual, can be placed in any cell to create a vertical and horizontal structure. Dreamweaver provides two ways to create tables: Standard view and Layout view. In both cases, once you've created a table, there are many ways you can manipulate it to get the exact look you want.

Note

Standard view is best suited for laying out tabular data or for simple organization of text and graphics. Layout view, on the other hand, is better suited for laying out your entire page.

Creating Tables in Standard View

The tools in Standard view let you lay out tabular data and organize text and graphics in your Document Window. As with many features in Dreamweaver, there are two ways to insert tables in Standard view. The first uses the Object Palette:

1. Place your cursor at the location in the Document Window where you want to insert the table.

2. If you don't already have the Object Palette open, go to Windows ➢ Objects, or use the shortcut Command+F2 (Macintosh) or Ctrl+F2 (Windows).

3. Make sure you have the Standard View button toggled on at the bottom of the Object Palette.

4. In the Common panel of the Object Palette (which is accessible by clicking the down-pointing arrow in the top-right corner of the Object Palette), click the Insert Table button.

5. Once the Insert Table dialog box appears, type in the values of your table. To set the initial properties of your table, skip forward to the next section ("Setting Initial Table Properties in Standard View").

To insert a table using the Insert menu, follow these steps:

1. In the Document Window, place your cursor where you want to insert the table.

2. Go to Insert ➤ Table, or use the shortcut Cmd+Option+T (Mac) or Ctrl+Alt+T (Win).

3. Once the Insert Table dialog box appears, type in the values of your table. To set the initial properties of your table, go to the next section ("Setting Initial Table Properties in Standard View").

Setting Initial Table Properties in Standard View

The Table Properties dialog box appears after you use either the Object Palette or the Insert menu to add your table. This dialog box allows you to set the initial properties of your table. You can either accept the default values (which can easily be changed later) or type in some of your own. You must go though this step for your table to be inserted into the Document Window. Let's have a look at each of the values in the Table Properties dialog box and how you change them.

Note

As we're dealing with each property separately, "Click OK" is given as the final step. While you can certainly click OK after setting any of the properties, you may want to set them all before clicking the OK button.

Setting Rows and Columns

When you set the number of rows and columns, you are essentially setting the structure of your table. Each value is represented numerically and is set like this:

1. With the Table Properties dialog box open (which should have automatically opened when you used either the Object Palette or the Insert menu to add a table), click your mouse in the Rows field.

2. Type in the number of rows you want in your table (for our purposes, let's enter 5).

3. Click your mouse in the Columns field.

4. Type in the number of columns you want in your table (for our purposes, let's enter 3).

5. Click OK.

Setting Table Width

Once you've set the amount of rows and columns, you need to set the width of your table. There are two types of width values you can choose from: pixels and percent. As is the case with Horizontal Rules (see Chapter 3, "Adding and Manipulating Text"), if you choose pixels, the width of your table will be fixed, regardless of the size of the user's browser window. As a result, if the width of the table is larger than the browser window, the user will have to scroll to see the entire table. On the other hand, if you choose percent, your table will always resize dynamically.

Warning

When you set the table size to percent, the objects in the cells determine the maximum size that your table can shrink.

These are the steps necessary to set the width of your table:

1. With the Table Properties dialog box open (which should have automatically opened when you used either the Object Palette or the Insert menu to add a table), click the down-pointing arrow to the right of the Width field to set your size either to pixels or percent. For our purposes, choose Percent.

Insert Table			
Rows: 5	Cell Padding:		OK
Columns: 3	Cell Spacing:		Cancel
Width: 75	Percent ▼		Help
	Percent		
Border: 1	Pixels		

2. Click your cursor in the Width field.

3. Enter a value for the width of your table (for our purposes, type in **75**).

4. Click OK.

Setting Border Thickness

The next step in setting your initial table properties is the border thickness, or the solid edge that runs around the perimeter of the table.

The table's border, whose value is set in pixels, can be any color you choose; the default color is gray. Don't worry, you can change the border color after you've already set the initial table properties.

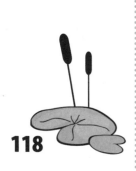

Tip

If you want your table to be invisible, simply set the border thickness to 0.

Follow these steps to set a table's border thickness:

1. With the Table Properties dialog box open (which should have automatically opened when you used the Object Palette or the Insert menu to add a table), click your cursor in the Border field.

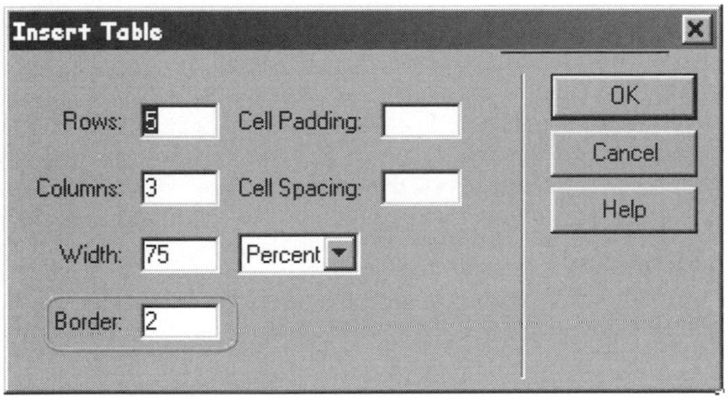
Insert Table
Rows: 5
Columns: 3
Width: 75
Percent
Border: 2
Cell Padding:
Cell Spacing:
OK
Cancel
Help

2. Type a value that you want for your border thickness (for our purposes, type in **1**).
3. Click OK.

Setting Cell Padding and Cell Spacing

Both cell padding and cell spacing can be tricky to get a handle on. Basically, cell padding refers to the number of pixels between the wall of the cell and the object within the cell.

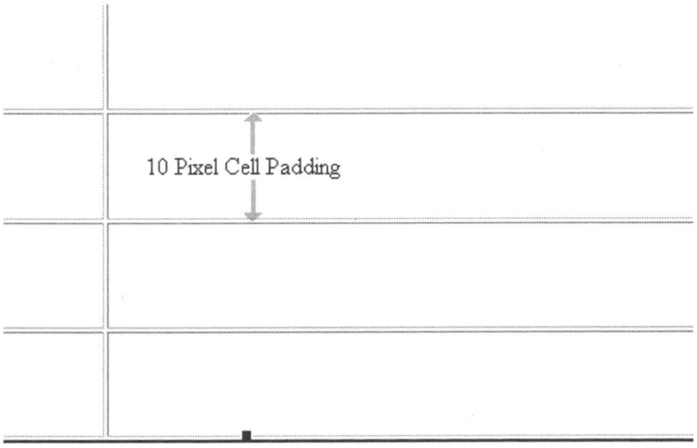
10 Pixel Cell Padding

Cell padding
Cell padding refers to the number of pixels between the wall of the cell and the object within the cell.

Cell spacing
Cell spacing is the number of pixels between each cell.

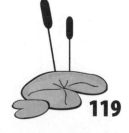

Cell spacing is the number of pixels between each cell.

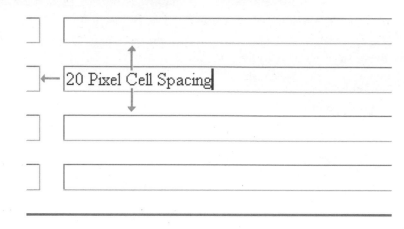

The value for both cell padding and cell spacing are in pixels. These are the necessary steps for setting cell padding and cell spacing:

1. With the Table Properties dialog box open (which should have automatically opened when you used the Object Palette or the Insert menu to add a table), click your cursor in the Cell Padding field.

2. Type in a value for your table's cell padding (for our purposes, enter **5**).

3. Click your cursor in the Cell Spacing field.

4. Type in a value that you want for your table's cell spacing (for our purposes, enter **5**).

5. Click OK.

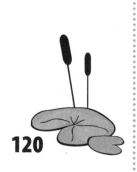

Manipulating Tables in Standard View

You can access and manipulate the properties of a table after you've created it by using the Property Inspector. Many of the initial table properties you set with the Table Properties dialog box are accessible, along with other properties such as table alignment and background color.

Setting Table Alignment

Like most elements in Dreamweaver (such as images and text), you can align a table to your page. As with any other alignment, you are limited to left, center, and right justification.

Warning

If your table width is set at 100%, aligning it won't make any difference.

1. Select the table you want to align.

Tip

To select the entire table, simply click its top-left corner, the right edge, or the bottom edge.

2. If you don't already have the Property Inspector open, go to Window ➤ Properties, or use the shortcut Cmd/Ctrl+F3.

3. Click the down-pointing arrow to the right of the Align field to open the Table Align drop-down menu.

Table Name	Rows 5	W 75	%	CellPad 5	Align Default
	Cols 3	H	pixels	CellSpace 5	Border 2

4. Choose from the Align options: Left, Right, Center.

Changing Background Color

Changing the background color of a table works pretty much the same as changing the background color of your page (see Chapter 2, "Setting Up a Dreamweaver Document"). The only difference, obviously, is that the color is confined to the table itself. If you resize the table (as we will shortly), the background color will automatically increase to fill the entire table. Follow these steps to change the background color of your table:

1. Select the table whose color you want to change.

2. If you don't already have the Property Inspector open, go to Window ➤ Properties, or use the shortcut Cmd/Ctrl+F3.

3. Click the color swatch directly to the right of the words "Bg Color" (in the expanded Property Inspector) to open the Color Palette.

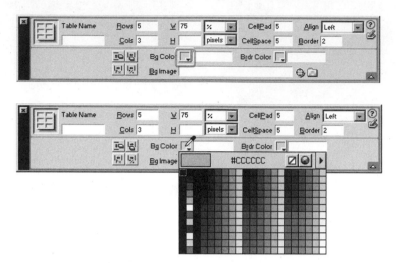

4. Move your mouse over a color you like and click it. Notice that the background color of your table automatically changes.

Tip

If you want to choose a color that isn't contained in the Color Palette, you can follow the procedure described in Chapter 2 (see the section "Using the Color Dialog Box").

Setting Border Color

As mentioned earlier in the section "Setting Border Thickness," you can change the border color as well as the thickness:

1. Select the table whose border color you want to change.

2. If you don't already have the Property Inspector open, go to Window ➢ Properties, or use the shortcut Cmd/Ctrl+F3.

3. Click the color swatch directly to the right of the words Brdr Color to open the Color Palette.

4. Move your mouse over a color you like and click it. Notice that the border color of your table automatically changes.

If your border thickness is set to 0, changing the border color won't have any visible effect. If you have your border thickness set to more than 0, you'll still be able to see the rows and columns after you've changed the table's background color. If you want your entire table to be one solid color, there are a couple of ways to do so. First, you could set your table border thickness to 0. Also, you could set your border color to the same color as the background of the table.

Adding a Background Image

As in the case of your web page, you can add a background image to a table. The only difference, obviously, is that the image is confined to the table itself. If you resize the table (as we will shortly), the background image will automatically fill its increased size.

Tip

When you add a background image to a table, the image tiles to fit the available space, the same as when you add a background image to a web page.

1. Select the table to which you want to add a background image.

2. If you don't already have the Property Inspector open, go to Window ➢ Properties, or use the shortcut Cmd/Ctrl+F3.

3. Click the browse Icon directly to the right of the Bg Image field.

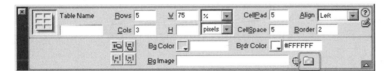

4. When the file navigation screen appears, locate and select the file you want to use as a background image in your table.

Warning

If you have both a background image and a background color set for your table, the background image will always cover the background color.

Resizing a Table

You certainly aren't stuck with the initial table width you set. These are the steps necessary to resize your table:

1. Select the table you want to resize.

2. If you don't already have the Property Inspector open, go to Window ➢ Properties, or use the shortcut Cmd/Ctrl+F3.

3. Click the drop-down menu to the right of the Width (W) field to choose either pixels or percent.

4. Click your cursor in the W field and type in a value for the width of your table.

5. Click your cursor in the H field and type in a value for the height of your table.

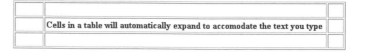

6. To apply your changes, hit Enter or click anywhere off of the Property Inspector in the Document Window.

Note

It isn't as important to set the Height value as it is to set the Width value, because a table will constantly expand vertically to fit the content you add in its cells.

Adding Text to a Table

Follow these steps to add text to a table:

1. Click your mouse in the cell where you want to add text.

2. Type the text you want to add. You'll notice that the cell automatically expands to accommodate what you're typing.

	Cells in a table will automatically expand to accomodate the text you type	

3. To move to the next cell, either click your mouse in the desired location or hit Tab.

Adding an Image to a Table

Follow these steps to add an image to your table:

1. Click your mouse in the cell where you want to add an image.

2. Click the Insert Image button in the Object Palette, or go to Insert ➤ Image (or use the shortcut Cmd+Opt+I/Ctrl+Alt+I).

3. When the navigation screen appears, locate and select the image you want to insert.

4. You'll notice that the cell automatically expands to accommodate the image.

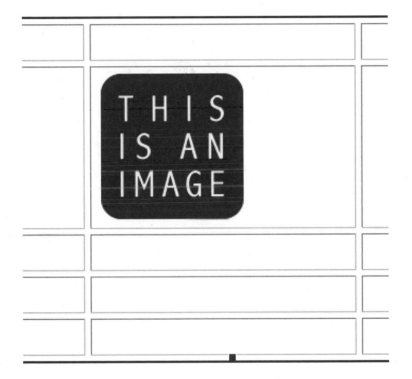

Working with Rows, Columns, and Cells

Now that you can apply changes to the table as a whole, you'll learn how to work with individual rows, columns, and cells.

Selecting Individual Rows or Columns

Before you learn how to work with individual rows, columns, and cells, you need to know how to select them (as opposed to selecting the entire table). Follow these steps to select an individual table row:

1. Position your cursor just to the left (outside the table border) of the row you want to select. Notice that the cursor changes to a right-pointing arrow.

2. Click your mouse to select the entire row.

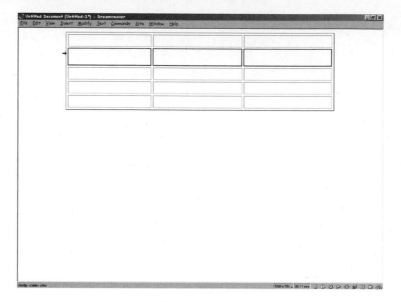

Follows these steps to select a column:

1. Position your cursor just above the column you want to select. Notice that the cursor changes to a down-pointing arrow.

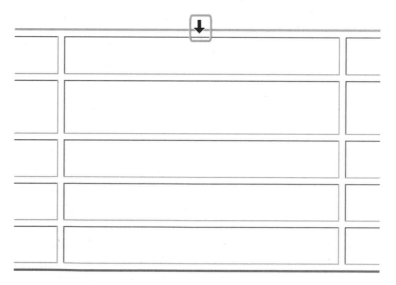

2. Click your mouse to select the entire column.

Adding a Row or Column

A table certainly wouldn't be much use if you were allowed to work only with a fixed number of rows and columns. We'll first add a row, and then move on to adding a column.

1. Select the table to which you want to add a row (or rows).

2. If you don't already have the Property Inspector open, go to Window ➢ Properties, or use the shortcut Cmd/Ctrl+F3.

3. Place your cursor in the Rows field.

4. Type in the total number of rows you want your table to have. For instance, if you have 3 rows and you want to add 3, you would type in **6**.

5. To apply your changes, either hit Enter or click off of the Property Inspector anywhere in the Document Window.

To add a column (or columns) to your table, the steps are almost the same:

1. Select that table to which you want to add a column (or columns).

2. If you don't already have the Property Inspector open, go to Window ➢ Properties, or use the shortcut Cmd/Ctrl+F3.

3. Place your cursor in the Cols (short for columns) field.

4. Type in the total number of columns you want your table to have. For instance, if you have 3 columns, and you want to add 3, you would type in **6**.

5. To apply your changes, either hit Enter or click off of the Property Inspector anywhere in the Document Window.

127

Deleting a Row or Column

Next, you'll learn how to delete a row (or rows), and then you'll move on to deleting columns.

1. Click your cursor in the cell of a row you want to delete.

2. Go to Modify ➢ Table ➢ Delete Row, or use the shortcut Cmd/Ctrl+Shift+M.

3. The row where you placed your cursor is automatically deleted.

To delete a column (or columns) to your table, the steps are almost the same:

1. Click your cursor in the cell of a column you want to delete.

2. Go to Modify ➢ Table ➢ Delete Column, or use the shortcut Cmd/Ctrl+Shift+-.

3. The column where you placed your cursor is automatically deleted.

Tip

You can also decrease the number of rows or columns in your table by following the procedure you used when adding rows or columns with the Property Inspector, but type in a smaller number instead of a larger one.

Aligning Content within a Cell

Because a cell is a unit unto itself, you have a few more alignment options than you normally would. While you can align content to the left, center, or right, you also can align content vertically to the top, middle, bottom, or baseline. This is handy when you want to exert a little more control over how the content in your table looks. Folllow these steps to align content within a cell:

1. Click your mouse in the cell whose contents you want to align. Make sure that your cursor is visible in the cell before you continue.

Tip

There is no need to select the object you want to align. You simply need to place your cursor in the cell you want to work with, and Dreamweaver will do the rest.

2. If you don't already have the Property Inspector open, go to Window ➤ Properties, or use the shortcut Cmd/Ctrl+F3.

3. To align contents horizontally, click the down-pointing arrow to the right of the Horz field.

4. Choose Left, Right, or Center according to your page's needs (for our purposes, choose Center).

5. You'll notice that the contents in the cell align automatically.

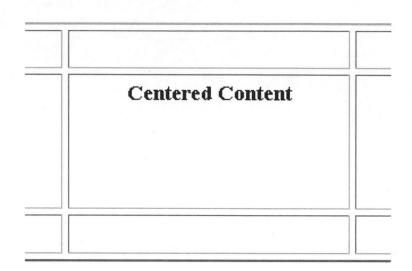

To align content vertically, the process is almost the same:

1. Click your mouse in the cell whose contents you want to align. Make sure that your cursor is visible in the cell before you continue.

2. If you don't already have the Property Inspector open, go to Window ➢ Properties, or use the shortcut Cmd/Ctrl+F3.

3. To align contents vertically, click the down-pointing arrow to the right of the Vert field.

4. Choose Top, Middle, Bottom, or Baseline according to your page's needs (for our purposes, choose Bottom).

5. As in the case of the horizontal alignment, you'll notice that the contents of the cell align automatically.

Warning

Once you set a cell's alignment (whether horizontal or vertical), all future content that you add will also be aligned this way.

Merging Cells

Because you're working with tables in Standard view, you aren't stuck with the symmetrical columns and rows that you initially created. You can merge any number of continuous cells into one "megacell," which allows you to exert more control over using a table to lay out content.

Warning

Besides being contiguous, the cells you want to merge must be in the shape of a rectangle.

1. Place your cursor in the first cell you want to include in your multicell selection.

2. Hold down Shift and click in the next cell you want to include in your selection. You'll notice that a black selection box appears around both cells.

3. With Shift still held down, click any other cells you want to include in your selection.

Note

Remember that the selection must be in the form of a rectangle. If it isn't, Dreamweaver will automatically expand the selection to make it a rectangle.

4. If you don't already have the Property Inspector open, go to Window ➢ Properties, or use the shortcut Cmd/Ctrl+F3.

5. Click the Merge Cells icon in the bottom-left corner of the expanded Property Inspector.

6. Your selected cells will automatically combine into one cell.

Creating Tables in Layout View

Layout view is probably one of the most progressive and useful new features in Dreamweaver. When using Layout view, you are creating tables, but you are creating them with a much higher level of control than you had in Standard view. Layout view allows you to draw tables and cells (called layout tables and layout cells) and then manipulate them. The result is a page laid out with much more precision. Once you've drawn a layout table or cell in Layout view, Dreamweaver takes care of the underlying table structure.

Inserting a Layout Table

When you insert a layout table, you are essentially drawing the external structure of your table. A layout table, however, doesn't have any internal structure until you draw layout cells within it. Let's take a look at how to insert a layout table:

1. If you don't already have the Object Palette open, go to Windows , Objects, or use the shortcut Cmd/Ctrl+F2.

2. Click the Layout View icon in the View panel at the bottom of the Object Palette.

3. Click the Draw Layout Table icon in the Layout panel of the Object Palette.

Layout tables

A table which is "drawn" in Layout view.

Layout cells
A cell that is "drawn" in Layout view. Unlike in Standard view, layout cells can be dynamically moved and resized within a layout table.

132

4. When you move your cursor off of the Object Palette, it will automatically change into a plus (+) symbol

5. Position the plus (+) cursor where you want to start your layout table.

Note

No matter where you place your cursor, Dreamweaver will automatically justify the layout table to the left and top of the Document Window.

6. Click your mouse button and drag until the outline is the size that you want for your layout table.

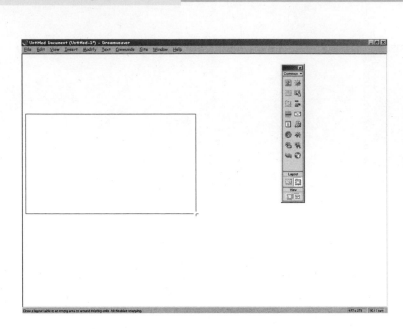

7. When the outline is the size you want, release your mouse button. The layout table is automatically created.

Inserting a Layout Cell

Layout cells cannot exist without a table in which to reside. If you draw a layout cell in Layout view, Dreamweaver will automatically create a layout table as a container for the cell.

Note

When you draw a layout cell, the layout table that is created by Dreamweaver automatically occupies the entire width of your Document Window.

1. If you don't already have the Object Palette open, go to Windows ➢ Objects, or use the shortcut Cmd/Ctrl+F2.

2. Click the Layout View icon in the View panel at the bottom of the Object Palette.

3. Click the Draw Layout Cell Icon in the Layout panel of the Object Palette.

4. When you move your cursor off of the Object Palette, it will automatically change into a plus (+) symbol.

5. Position the plus (+) cursor where you want to start your layout cell.

Note

Unlike a layout table, which is always justified to the top and left of the Document Window, you can draw a layout cell anywhere you want.

6. Click your mouse button and drag until the outline is the size that you want for your layout cell.

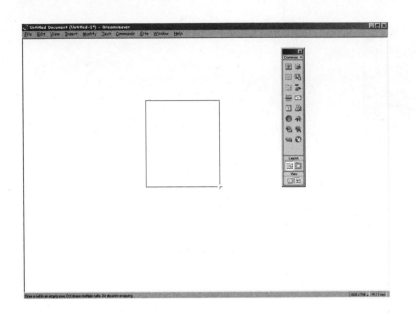

7. When the outline is the size you want, release your mouse button and the layout cell will be automatically created. Notice that not only is the layout cell created, but the underlying structure of the layout table is created as well.

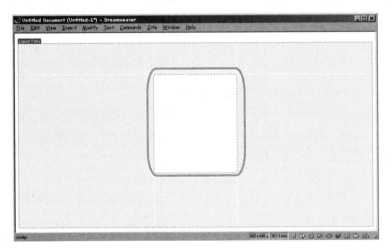

If you already have a layout table inserted, you can simply follow the steps outlined above to draw any number of layout cells within its confines.

Moving and Resizing Layout Tables and Cells

Both layout cells and tables can be resized. On the other hand, while layout cells can be moved around (which is one of their strengths), layout tables are pretty much stuck where you initially place them. This section will look at how to resize a layout table and then how to resize and move layout cells.

Resizing a Layout Table

Follow these steps to resize a layout table:

1. Select the layout table you want to resize by clicking either its edge or the Layout Table tab.

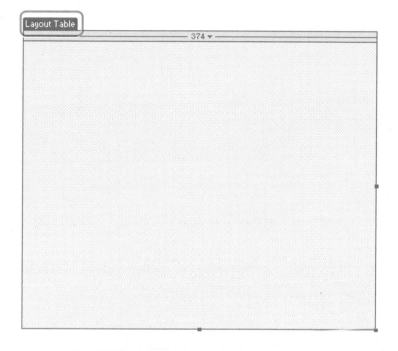

2. Once you do this, resize handles will appear around the table's edge.

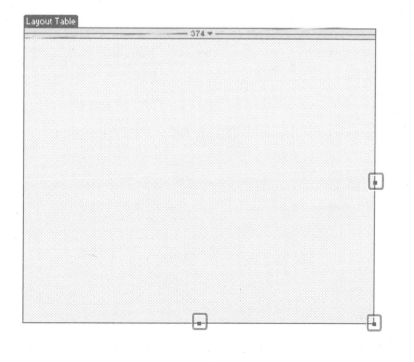

3. Click one of the handles and drag the table to the desired size.

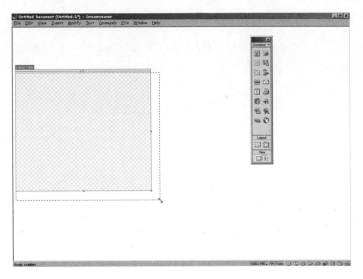

4. Release the handle when the table has reached the desired size.

Warning

A layout table cannot be resized any smaller than the layout cells that it contains.

Resizing a Layout Cell

Follow these steps to resize a layout cell:

1. Select the layout cell you want to resize by clicking its edge. (You'll notice that the edge of this layout cell will change color from blue to red when you move your mouse over it.)

2. After clicking the cell's edge, the resize handles will appear.

3. Click one of the handles and drag the cell to the desired size.

Warning

You can't increase the size of a layout cell beyond the edge of the layout table.

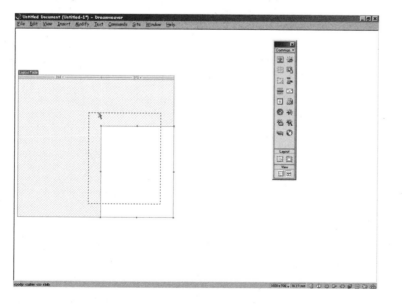

4. Release the handle when the cell has reached the desired size.

Moving a Layout Cell

Unlike a layout table, you can move a layout cell. Follow these steps:

1. Select the layout cell you want to move by clicking its edge. (You'll notice that the edge of this layout cell will change color from blue to red when you move your mouse over it.)

2. With your mouse still on the cell's edge, click your mouse button and drag it to where you want to move the cell.

3. When the layout cell is where you want it, release your mouse button.

139

Warning
You can't move the layout cell outside the confines of the layout table.

Manipulating a Layout Table with the Property Inspector

Once you've created a layout table, you can access several of its properties using the Property Inspector. This section will look at changing a layout table's width and height, as well as changing its cell padding and cell spacing.

Setting Width and Height

Instead of resizing a table by dragging, the Property Inspector allows you to set the exact width and height of any layout table in pixels:

1. Select the layout table you want to resize by either clicking its edge or the Layout Table tab.

2. If you don't already have the Property Inspector open, go to Window ➢ Properties, or use the shortcut Cmd/Ctrl+F3.

3. Make sure the Fixed radio button to the left of the Width field is checked.

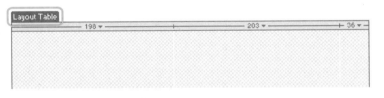

4. Click your mouse in the Width field and enter a value. As soon as you enter it and move your cursor out of the field, your changes take effect.

140

5. Click your mouse in the Height field (you can also hit the Tab button once) and enter a value. As soon as you enter it and move your cursor out of the field, your changes take effect.

Setting Cell Padding and Spacing

Here's how to set a table's cell padding and cell spacing in Layout view:

1. Select the layout table you are working with by either clicking its edge or the Layout Table tab.

2. If you don't already have the Property Inspector open, go to Window ➤ Properties, or use the shortcut Cmd/Ctrl+F3.

3. Click in the CellPad field (short for cell padding) and enter the value you want for your layout table.

4. Click your mouse in the CellSpace field (you can instead hit the Tab key once) and enter the value you want for your layout table's cell spacing.

5. To apply your changes, either hit Enter or click your cursor anywhere off of the Property Inspector in the Document Window.

Note

If you don't have any layout cells in your layout table, your changes will not be visible until some are added.

Manipulating a Layout Cell with the Properties Inspector

As in the case of a layout table, changing the properties of a layout cell with the Property Inspector gives you far more control over its properties than when it was initially created. In this section, you'll learn how to set the height and width of a layout cell and change its background color and internal alignment.

Setting Width and Height

When you initially create layout cells, you really don't have pixel-precise control over their size. If you use the Property Inspector, however, you can set the exact size of any layout cell. Just follow these steps:

1. Select the layout cell whose width and height you want to set by clicking its edge. You'll notice that the edge of the layout cell will change color from blue to red when you move your mouse over it.

2. If you don't already have the Property Inspector open, go to Window ➤ Properties, or use the shortcut Cmd/Ctrl+F3.

3. Make sure the Fixed radio button to the left of the Width field is checked.

4. Click your mouse in the Width field and enter a value in pixels. As soon as you enter it and move your cursor out of the field, your changes take effect.

5. Click your mouse in the Height field (you can also hit the Tab button once) and enter a value in pixels. As soon as you enter it and move your cursor out of the field, your changes take effect.

Setting a Background Color

By changing the background color of your layout cells in Layout view, you can get some genuinely interesting page layouts. To do so, follow these steps:

1. Select the layout cell whose background color you want to change by clicking its edge. You'll notice that the edge of the layout cell will change color from blue to red when you move your mouse over it.

2. If you don't already have the Property Inspector open, go to Window ≻ Properties, or use the shortcut Cmd/Ctrl+F3.

3. Click the color swatch directly to the right of Bg to open the Color Palette.

4. Move your mouse over a color you like and click it. Notice that the background color of your layout cell automatically changes.

Setting Internal Alignment

You can align content within a layout cell in much the same way as you do when you align content within a cell in Standard view. Follow these steps:

1. Select the layout cell whose content you want to align by clicking its edge. You'll notice that the edge of the layout cell will change color from blue to red when you move your mouse over it.

2. If you don't already have the Property Inspector open, go to Window ≻ Properties, or use the shortcut Cmd/Ctrl+F3.

Tip

As with cells in Standard view, you don't need to select the object you want to align. You simply need to place your cursor in the cell you want to work with, and Dreamweaver will do the rest.

3. To align contents horizontally, click the down-pointing arrow to the right of the Horz field.

4. Choose Left, Right, or Center according to your layout cell's needs (for our purposes, choose Right).

5. You'll notice that the cell's contents align automatically.

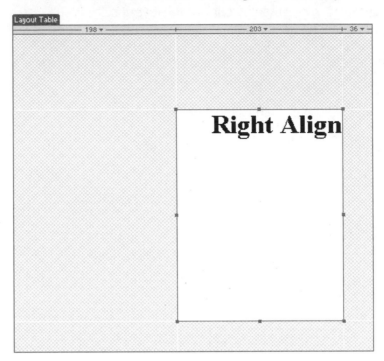

To align content vertically, the process is almost the same:

1. Select the layout cell whose content you want to align by clicking its edge. You'll notice that the edge of the layout cell will change color from blue to red when you move your mouse over it.

2. If you don't already have the Property Inspector open, go to Window ➢ Properties, or use the shortcut Cmd/Ctrl+F3.

3. To align contents vertically, click the down-pointing arrow to the right of the Vert field.

4. Choose Top, Middle, Bottom, or Baseline according to your layout cell's needs (for our purposes, choose Bottom).

5. You'll notice that the cell's contents align automatically.

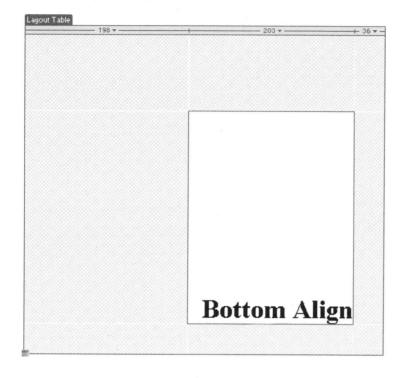

Warning

Once you set a layout cell's alignment (whether horizontal or vertical), all added content will also be aligned this way.

Summary

This chapter explored creating and working with tables. First it looked at creating and manipulating them in Standard view. It then delved into creating and manipulating tables in Layout view, a new (and terribly cool!) feature in Dreamweaver 4.

Part 4

First Steps with Fireworks

This section of the book will take a look at the fundamentals you need to know before creating images in Fireworks. We'll start by exploring the Fireworks interface, then move on to creating a new document and setting the initial document properties. Finally, we'll look at how to import graphics files from other applications.

First Steps with Fireworks

Chapter 7

Before You Get Started with Fireworks

As in Dreamweaver, once you double-click Firework's program icon, you'll be immediately faced with a host of windows and palettes. In this chapter, you'll learn exactly what Fireworks is and what it can do for you. Finally, you'll learn how to navigate and work with the Fireworks interface. Topics in this chapter include the following:

- ◆ About Fireworks

- ◆ The Fireworks interface

Introducing Fireworks

While the web is a visual medium, web graphics are not like ordinary computer graphics. Issues such as color, file type, and file size make creating and managing web graphics a unique process. Most of the early versions of such graphics programs as Adobe Photoshop or Metacreations Painter (which is now owned by Corel) were not really equipped to deal with the specific needs of designing web graphics.

In March of 1998, Macromedia announced that it was releasing Fireworks, the first production tool that provided a unified environment for creating, optimizing, and producing high-quality graphics for the web. The program boasted a multitude of tools that not only allowed designers to tailor their graphics specifically for the web, but also gave designers the ability to create some pretty snazzy web features (such as rollovers and GIF animations). To top it all off, Fireworks's image-creating and manipulation tools, which were geared toward creating both bitmap and vector images, rivaled those of other graphics programs.

Four versions later, Fireworks has only gotten better.

Note

In Fireworks 4, Macromedia has introduced improvements that fall into five general categories: usability, image editing, animation, graphic design, HTML/export, and file format support. For a more detailed list of the improvements in each category, check out the exclusive web-only content for this book at www.sybex.com. Search for "Watrall."

Touring the Fireworks Interface

One of the most powerful features of Fireworks is its interface. The program boasts an incredible set of tools, all of which are instantly accessible. The interface, which is designed to accommodate a wide range of expertise and working styles, allows you to maximize what's really important: creativity. The interface itself is broken up into a series of panels and toolbars. In this section, we're going to take a look at the most common of these tools.

Exploring the Document Window

The Document Window is the canvas upon which you will paint your creations, the stage upon which you will make them dance and move. More than this, however, the Document Window is a tool in itself. Like the Document Window in Dreamweaver, it contains a number of very useful tools and information that will ultimately aid your creative process. Unlike Dreamweaver's, however, Fireworks's Document Window doesn't automatically open when you launch the program; you'll want to set the initial properties (like dimensions, color, and resolution) of each document you'll be working on.

To open up a new document follow these steps:

1. Select File ➢ New, or use the shortcut Command+N (Macintosh) or Ctrl+N (Windows).

2. This will open the New Document dialog box. For our purposes, just hit OK.

Note

If you simply hit OK in the New Document dialog box and don't set any initial document properties, Fireworks will create a new document that has a dimension of 500 x 500 pixels with a white background. This might not be exactly what you want, but it will definitely help you explore the Document Window.

The Preview Tabs

You'll notice that there are four tabs at the top of the Document Window: Original, Preview, 2-Up, and 4-Up.

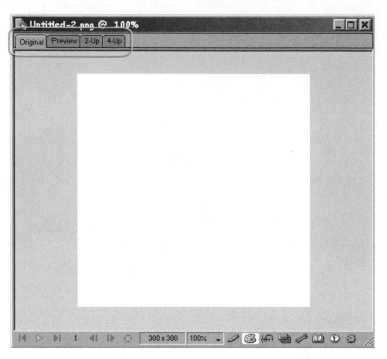

Each of these tabs represents a specific view of the current document in the Document Window. When you click the Original tab, the PNG version of the working image is displayed in the Document Window.

Note

PNG stands for Portable Network Graphic and is the native file format of Fireworks. For further information on PNGs, refer to the discussion of web file formats in Chapter 4, "Working with Images."

When you click the Preview tab, the graphic appears as it would in a web browser, based on current export settings. (For an in-depth look at export settings, see Chapter 11, "Optimizing and Exporting Images.")

The 2-Up tab gives you a side-by-side comparison of the original image and a preview of the image as it would look in a web browser at the current export settings. Basically, it shows you what you would see by clicking the Original tab and then the Preview tab, but it presents them simultaneously.

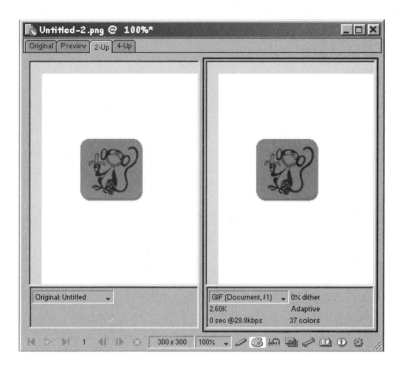

Finally, the 4-Up tab is basically the same as the 2-Up tab, but it displays two extra panels in which you can experiment with how your image will look at various export settings.

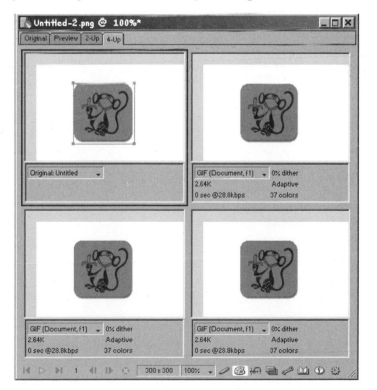

Note

To learn more about optimization, export, and how to take full advantage of the preview tabs, flip forward to Chapter 11.

The Mini-Launcher

Located at the bottom right-hand corner of the Document Window, the Mini-Launcher contains icons for opening and closing your most frequently used panels, including the Stroke, Layers, Behaviors, and Optimize panels.

Set Magnification

Somewhere along the line, you will probably want to magnify your document to do some detailed work or to get a better look at a particular section. Instead of using the Magnifying Glass tool, you can actually increase the magnification of your document by using the Set Magnification tool in the bottom-right section of the Document Window.

Untitled-2.png @ 100%*

| Original | Preview | 2-Up | 4-Up | GIF (Document.f1) |

300 x 300   100%

All you need to do is click the Set Magnification tool and choose the desired magnification from the drop-down menu.

```
    6%
   12%
   25%
   50%
   100%
✓  200%
   400%
   800%
  1600%
  3200%
  6400%
```

Page Preview

The Page Preview tool allows you quick access to basic information (including document width, height, and resolution) about your current open document.

If you click this tool, you get a handy pop-up display of information about your document.

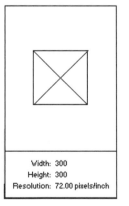

Object

Any item, such as a rectangle, ellipse, or text, that you create in Fireworks.

Using the Toolbox

The Toolbox contains many tools that allow you to create, select, and edit objects. During the process of image creation, you'll find that the tools in the Toolbox are absolutely indispensable. The Toolbox opens by default when you launch Fireworks. If you've closed it down, just go to Window ➢ Tools to reopen it.

Tip

When the Toolbox is open, a checkmark will be displayed next to its name in the Window menu. So, if you can't see your Toolbox and the Window menu is indicating that it's open, it might be "buried" under several other things. Try locating it by moving things around in your workspace.

The Toolbox includes dozens of tools, some of which are arranged in tool groups. A tool group includes several tools that share the same space in the Toolbox with other similar tools. A tool group is identified by a small down-pointing arrow in the lower right-hand corner of a tool icon in the Toolbox.

To access a tool in a tool group that isn't currently visible in the Toolbox, simply click the tool group's currently active tool and hold down your mouse button for several seconds. A pop-up menu will appear with the other tools in the tool group. Move your mouse over the tool you want to select, and release your mouse button. Once you've done this, the tool will automatically appear in the Toolbox.

Note

The specifics of what many of the tools do will be discussed in the coming chapters.

Using the Main Toolbar

In an effort to reduce the clutter of the working environment, the Main toolbar exists as a floating palette.

Tip

If you don't want to use the Main toolbar because it clutters up your workspace, you can access all of its functions through either the File or Edit menus.

To open the Main toolbar, select Window ➢ Toolbars ➢ Main. The toolbar contains the New, Save, Open, Import, Export, Print, Undo, Cut, Copy, and Paste commands.

Accessing the Modify Toolbar

As in the case of the Main toolbar, the Modify toolbar exists as a floating palette. (However, if you don't want to use the Modify toolbar because it clutters up your workspace, all of its functions are accessible through the Modify menu.) To access the Modify toolbar, go to Window ➢ Toolbars ➢ Modify.

Note

Mac users don't have access to a floating Modify toolbar. All of the commands, however, are accessible through the Modify menu.

The toolbar itself contains (from left to right) these commands: Group, Ungroup, Join, Split, Bring to Front, Bring Forward, Send Backward, Send to Back, Align, Rotate 90° Counterclockwise, Rotate 90° Clockwise, Flip Horizontally, and Flip Vertically.

Note

To learn more about the tools in the Modify toolbar, refer to Mastering Dreamweaver 4 and Fireworks 4 by David Crowder and Ronda Crowder (Sybex, 2001).

Using the Panels

Panels are floating controls that allow you to manipulate or add to a selected object. Because panels are floating tools, they are both draggable and dockable. Upon launching Fireworks, you'll find that most panels reside in a window with other similar panels. For example, the Color Table panel resides with the Color Mixer panel, the Swatches panel, the Optimize panel, and the Options panel. These panels make what is called the Color Table group. Because the panels themselves are dockable, you can alter the various groups. However, because similar panels are grouped together, you may want to leave them as they are.

Tip

For an explanation of how to dock palettes, refer to Chapter 1, "Starting Up Dreamweaver." The process for docking palettes in Fireworks is the same as in Dreamweaver.

In this section, you'll learn how to access the various panels that you'll learn to use in future chapters.

Tip

We won't cover the more advanced panels here. If you are curious about these panels, you should explore them using the Help features in Fireworks.

The Optimize Panel

With the Optimize panel, you can change the export values for your images. You can set the file format, manipulate the number of colors, set the level of transparency, choose a color palette, and alter a variety of other parameters.

To access the Optimize panel (if it isn't already open), go to Window ➤ Optimize. You can also click the Show Optimize button in the Document Window's Mini-Launcher to open the Optimize panel.

The Effects Panel

With the Effects panel, you can apply special effects such as drop shadow, blur, and glow to any object you desire. After having applied an effect, you can manipulate the parameters of the applied effect with the Effects panel itself.

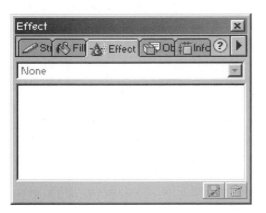

To access the Optimize panel (if it isn't already open), simply go to Window ➢ Effects, or use the shortcut Option/Alt+E.

The Color Table

The Color Table panel, which is part of a group of similar panels called the Color Table group, displays the colors that are currently being used in theyour working image on which you're working. The Color Table itself really only works only for images that use less than 256 individual colors. As a result, it will only be useful in only a small number of the images that you'll work with in Fireworks.

If you are working with an image that contains less than 256 colors, you can use the Color Table to alter the value of a particular color, add colors, delete colors, or set transparency.

If the Color Table isn't already open, you can access it by selecting Window ➢ Color Table.

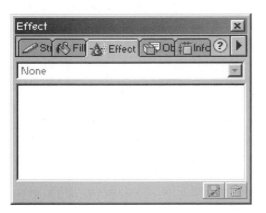

The Swatches Panel

Part of the Color Table group, the Swatches panel, opposed to showing only the currently used colors, displays a list of all the available colors, not only the ones being currently used. The exact colors displayed are determined by the current settings of the Swatches panel. For example, the colors displayed when the Swatches panel is set to Windows System will be different from those displayed if you've set the Swatches panel to Macintosh System.

To access the Swatches panel, simply follow this step: go to Window ➢ Swatches, or use the shortcut Cmd/Ctrl+F9.

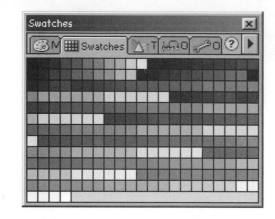

The Color Mixer

The Color Mixer panel is the third tool in the Color Table group that deals explicitly with color. Essentially, the Color Mixer lets you set the color system upon which your image is based upon. Your choices include **RGB** (red-green-blue), **CMY** (cyan-magenta-yellow), **HSB** (hue-saturation-brilliance), **hexadecimal**, and **grayscale**. Within these color systems, the Color Mixer allows you to mix (hence the name) your own custom colors.

If the Color Mixer isn't already open, all you have to do to is select Window ➢ Color Mixer, or use the shortcut Shift+F5.

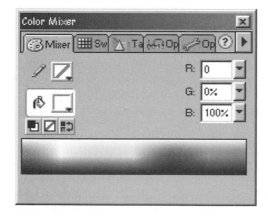

You can also access the Color Mixer by clicking the Show Mixer button in the Document Window's Mini-Launcher.

The Layers Panel

The Layers panel in Fireworks is similar to those found in other graphics programs such as Adobe Photoshop or Macromedia FreeHand. It's easiest to think of a layer as an invisible level where you can create and place objects. Layers enable you to split your artwork when

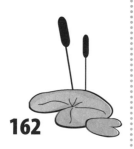

you're building complicated or composite images. Different portions of the image can exist in different layers and be selectively turned off or on so that you can isolate just the portion you are working on. Generally speaking, layers are a great way to manage and control the creation and composition of an image.

To open the Layers panel, select Window ➢ Layers, or use the shortcut F2.

You can also access the Layers panel by clicking the Show Layers button in the Document Window's Mini-Launcher.

The Frames Panel

The Frames panel is the primary tool you'll use when composing animations. It contains all of the various frames that make up your animation, and allows you to add, delete, and manipulate frames.

To access the Frames panel, select Window ➢ Frames, or use the shortcut Shift+F2.

The Stroke Panel

The Stroke panel is used to set the brush stroke for any path-creating tool such as the pen, ellipse, or brush. With the Stroke panel, you can access various parameters of the stroke, including texture, stroke category, stroke name, brush size, brush color, and stroke size.

To access the Stroke panel, go to Window ➤ Stroke, or use the shortcut Cmd+Opt+F4 (Mac) or Ctrl+Alt+F4 (Win).

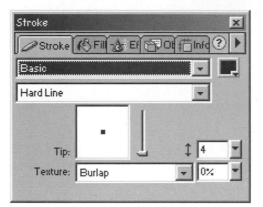

The Fill Panel

Gradient

A gradient is a gradual transition from one color to another.

Fills are applied to the interior of an object to give it a color, a color gradient, a texture, or a pattern. You can use the Fill panel to apply fills and to set characteristics such as the fill edge.

To access the Fill panel, select Window ➤ Fills, or use the shortcut Shift+F7.

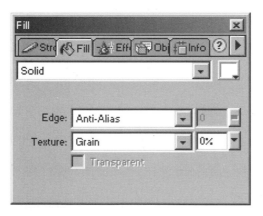

The Styles Panel

A style is a predetermined set of strokes, fills, and textures that can be applied to an object with one action (opposed to many). While Fireworks actually comes with a library of styles, the program also allows you to create your own styles.

To access the Styles panel, go to Window ➢ Styles, or use the shortcut Shift+F11.

Summary

This chapter introduced Fireworks and the features of the Fireworks interface. It explored the Document Window, the Toolbox, the Main toolbar, the Modify toolbar, and various panels. This chapter introduced you to the basics of these tools and panels in preparation for explorations of their inner workings in future chapters.

Chapter 8

Setting Up a Fireworks Document

Now that you're familiar with the workings of the Fireworks interface and the Document Window, you'll learn how to set up your first Fireworks document. In this chapter, you'll learn how to set the initial properties for a new document. Further, you'll learn how to open an existing document. Finally, you'll look at how to open various image types in Fireworks. Topics in this chapter include:

- Opening a new document

- Setting initial document properties

- Opening an existing file

- Opening multiple files

- Opening non-Fireworks image files

Opening a New Document

Unlike in Dreamweaver where a new document is automatically opened when you start the program, you'll need to go through a few steps to open a new Fireworks document. The first step is to tell Fireworks that you want to start a new document (as opposed to opening an existing one). To open a new document, select File ➢ New, or use the shortcut Command+N (Macintosh) or Ctrl+N (Windows).

Setting Document Properties

After using the File drop-down menu to tell Fireworks that you want to start working on a new document, you'll be immediately faced with the New Document dialog box. This is where you set the initial page properties of the document you want to create, including the document dimensions, document resolution, and canvas color.

Resolution

Resolution is the quality of a viewed image either on a computer screen or printed output. In most cases, resolution is measured in dots per inch (dpi). Generally speaking, the higher the dpi the better the resolution.

New Document

Canvas Size: 976.6K

Width: 500 — Pixels — W: 500

Height: 500 — Pixels — H: 500

Resolution: 72 — Pixels/Inch

Canvas Color:
- ○ White
- ● Transparent
- ○ Custom

OK   Cancel

Note

In each of the next sections, I've included "Click OK" as the final step. However, if you're setting the initial page properties for the first time, you will probably want to go through each stage (setting dimensions, setting resolution, and setting canvas color) before you hit OK and create the new document.

Setting Document Dimensions

The first thing you need to do when setting your initial page properties is to tell Fireworks the dimensions of your new document. To do this, just follow these steps:

1. If the New Document dialog box isn't open, go to File ➤ New, or use the shortcut Cmd/Ctrl+N.

2. Open the drop-down menu to the right of the Width field and choose a unit of measurement to represent the width of your new document. (Most users choose pixels over centimeters or inches.)

New Document

Canvas Size: 976.6K

Width: 500 | Pixels | W: 500

Height: 500 | Pixels | H: 500

Resolution: 72 | Pixels/Inch

Canvas Color:
- ○ White
- ● Transparent
- ○ Custom

OK | Cancel

3. In the Width field, enter a value for the width of your new document.

New Document

Canvas Size: 976.6K

Width: 500 | Pixels | W: 500

Height: 500 | Pixels | H: 500

Resolution: 72 | Pixels/Inch

Canvas Color:
- ○ White
- ● Transparent
- ○ Custom

OK | Cancel

4. Open the drop-down menu to the right of the Height field and choose a unit of measurement to represent the height of your new document.

New Document

Canvas Size: 976.6K

Width: 500   Pixels ▼   W: 500

Height: 500   Pixels ▼   H: 500

Resolution: 72   Pixels/Inch ▼

Canvas Color:

○ White
● Transparent
○ Custom ▣

OK   Cancel

5. In the Height field, enter a value for the height of your new document.

New Document

Canvas Size: 976.6K

Width: 500   Pixels ▼   W: 500

Height: 500   Pixels ▼   H: 500

Resolution: 72   Pixels/Inch ▼

Canvas Color:

○ White
● Transparent
○ Custom ▣

OK   Cancel

6. Click OK.

Tip

If you want to change the dimensions of your canvas after setting them with the New Document dialog box, go to Modify ➣ Canvas Size and make the changes you want.

Setting Document Resolution

When you are setting document resolution, you are essentially telling Fireworks how many pixels per unit of measurement (either inch or centimeter) your image will have. A higher resolution means that you've got more pixels squashed into every inch of your image (or centimeter). More pixels squashed in every inch (or centimeter) of your image means that your image will have a higher resolution and, therefore, look better.

Tip

The web only displays images that have a resolution of 72 dpi (for Windows machines) or 92 dpi (for Macintosh machines). So, if you are creating an image specifically for the web, it's really a waste of time to set your document resolution any higher than 72 dpi (because this is the lowest common denominator). You can set a higher resolution, but when you export and optimize your images, they'll end up with a resolution of 72 dpi anyway.

To set the resolution of your new document, follow these steps:

1. If the New Document dialog box isn't open, go to File ➢ New, or use the shortcut Cmd/Ctrl+N.

2. Use the drop-down menu to the right of the Resolution field to choose either pixels/inch or pixels/centimeter.

![New Document dialog box showing Canvas Size: 976.6K with Width: 500 Pixels (W: 500), Height: 500 Pixels (H: 500), Resolution: 72 Pixels/Inch, and Canvas Color options: White, Transparent (selected), Custom, with OK and Cancel buttons.]

3. Enter a value in the Resolution field.

```
New Document                                    [X]
┌─ Canvas Size: 976.6K ──────────────────────────┐
│                                                 │
│      Width:  [500]    [Pixels        ▼]  W: 500 │
│                                                 │
│      Height: [500]    [Pixels        ▼]  H: 500 │
│                                                 │
│   Resolution: [72]    [Pixels/Inch   ▼]         │
│                                                 │
├─ Canvas Color: ─────────────────────────────────┤
│   ○ White                                       │
│   ⊙ Transparent                                 │
│   ○ Custom        [■]                           │
│                                                 │
│                        [   OK   ]  [ Cancel ]   │
└─────────────────────────────────────────────────┘
```

4. Click OK.

Setting Document Canvas Color

The final step in setting your initial document properties is choosing a color for your canvas. To create a document that has a white canvas, follow these steps:

1. If the New Document dialog box isn't open, go to File ➢ New, or use the shortcut Cmd/Ctrl+N.

2. Click the radio button just to the left of the word "White."

```
New Document                                    [X]
┌─ Canvas Size: 976.6K ──────────────────────────┐
│                                                 │
│      Width:  [500]    [Pixels        ▼]  W: 500 │
│                                                 │
│      Height: [500]    [Pixels        ▼]  H: 500 │
│                                                 │
│   Resolution: [72]    [Pixels/Inch   ▼]         │
│                                                 │
├─ Canvas Color: ─────────────────────────────────┤
│   ⊙ White                                       │
│   ○ Transparent                                 │
│   ○ Custom        [■]                           │
│                                                 │
│                        [   OK   ]  [ Cancel ]   │
└─────────────────────────────────────────────────┘
```

3. Click OK.

To set your canvas to transparent, just do the following:

1. If the New Document dialog box isn't open, go to File ➢ New, or use the shortcut Cmd/Ctrl+N.

2. Click the radio button just to the left of the word "Transparent."

New Document		✕
Canvas Size: 976.6K		
Width: 500	Pixels ▼	W: 500
Height: 500	Pixels ▼	H: 500
Resolution: 72	Pixels/Inch ▼	
Canvas Color:		
○ White		
◉ Transparent		
○ Custom ▣		
	OK	Cancel

3. Click OK.

Tip

Use a transparent canvas if you are going to export your image as a transparent GIF or a PNG with transparency.

Instead of being a solid color, you'll notice that a canvas that you've set to transparent is a gray and white checkerboard pattern. Don't worry, this is just the symbol used to denote transparency. When you export your image, that checkerboard pattern won't be visible at all.

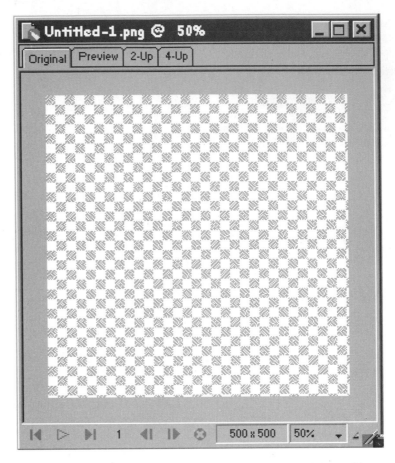

You can also choose a custom color for your canvas. Just follow these steps:

1. If the New Document dialog box isn't open, go to File ➢ New, or use the short-cut Cmd/Ctrl+N.

2. Click the radio button just to the left of the word "Custom."

A Dreamweaver and Fireworks Gallery

The following section is a gallery of web sites that have been created either in part or as a whole with Dreamweaver or Fireworks. They include examples from entertainment sites, a print publication site, an advertising firm, corporate communications and digital design firms, and an educational institution site.

The Matrix
www.matrixmag.com

Matrixmag.com is the online home of MATRIX, a literary and visual arts organization in Bloomington, Indiana. Dedicated to providing consistent public forums for area literary and visual arts, matrixmag.com merges excellent visual design with RealAudio recordings to push the limits of the contemporary art of spoken word.

Designed by Nathan Letsinger entirely in Dreamweaver and Fireworks, matrixmag.com uses clean design and effective navigation that encourages exploration and accessibility.

Copyright © 2000 Matrix. MATRIX—a space for literary and visual arts.

By creatively employing a very limited palette of colors and highly stylized graphics, matrixmag.com effectively evokes a feeling of beat poetry circa the 1960s.

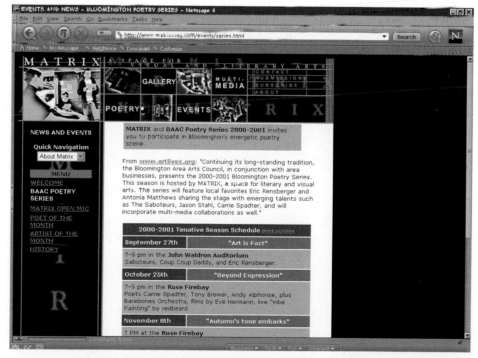

Copyright © 2000 Matrix. MATRIX—a space for literary and visual arts.

Doug Chiang Studio
www.dchiang.com

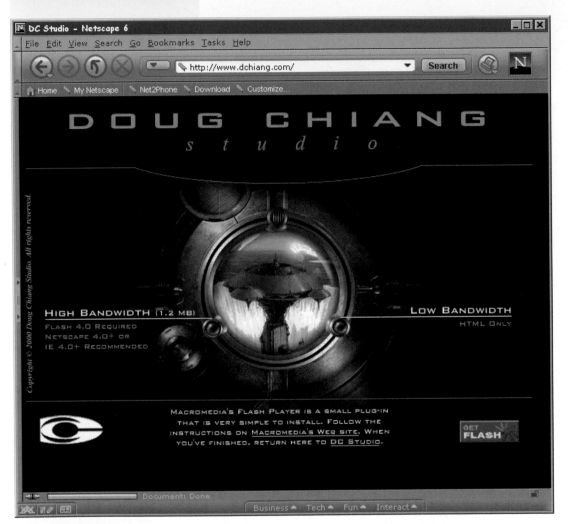

Copyright © Doug Chiang, DC Studio.

Founded by Doug Chiang, head of the Art department and Design Director for the Star Wars prequels, Doug Chiang Studio is currently working on a film/book project called *Robota: Reign of Machines*. The web site is intended to cater to those fascinated by the incredible work of Doug Chiang, as well as publicize and explore the studio's current project *Robota*: *Reign of Machines*.

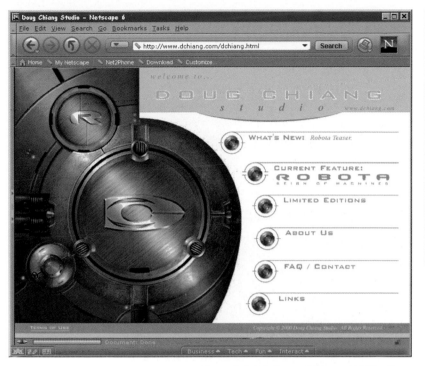

Designed using a combination of Dreamweaver and Fireworks (along with several other software packages), the web site combines Doug Chiang's beautiful and compelling style of illustration with a highly intuitive navigation scheme to create an exceptionally immersive experience.

Copyright © Doug Chiang, DC Studio.

Robota: Reign of Machines is a 160-page "film format" Illustrated book, due to be published in 2002, that explores the relationship between technology and nature against the backdrop of a futuristic society. The *Robota* section of the Doug Chiang Studio web site combines incredible illustration and immersive navigation to allow the user to explore the world of *Robota*.

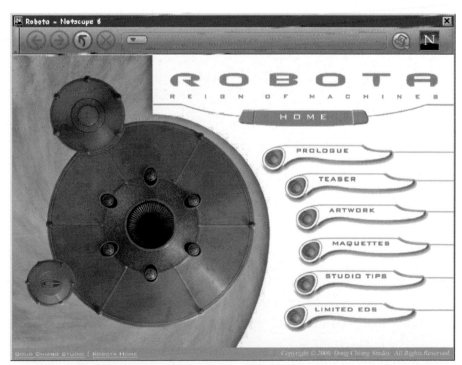

Copyright © Doug Chiang, DC Studio.

Terra Incognita

www.terraincognita.com

Copyright © 2000 Terra Incognita.

Widely recognized as one of the most talented and creative digital design firms in the industry, Terra Incognita believes that effective web sites are planned story-spaces that employ interactive narratives to engage the imagination. To help the development of vibrant interactive projects, their staff combines expertise in strategy, design, and technology with a strong foundation in the liberal arts.

Terra Incognita's web site uses colors and images that encourage a feeling of exploration and discovery. Their portfolio, which includes award-winning web sites for National Geographic and the Smithsonian Museum, embodies this feeling, and encourages the user to embark on an exhilarating intellectual journey.

Copyright © 2000 Terra Incognita.

Terra Incognita's team uses Dreamweaver's Check In/Check Out feature to help manage file sharing during the production process.

Copyright © 2000 Terra Incognita.

ONE

www.onemedia.com

Onemedia.com is the digital arm of ONE, a cross-cultural, bicoastal, print and online magazine covering design, culture, and innovation. ONE highlights the importance of design in the world today, ranging from rare inspiration to everyday brilliance.

Designed by Red Industries (www.redindustries.com) using a combination of Dreamweaver and Fireworks, onemedia.com exhibits a very clean design and stylish navigation.

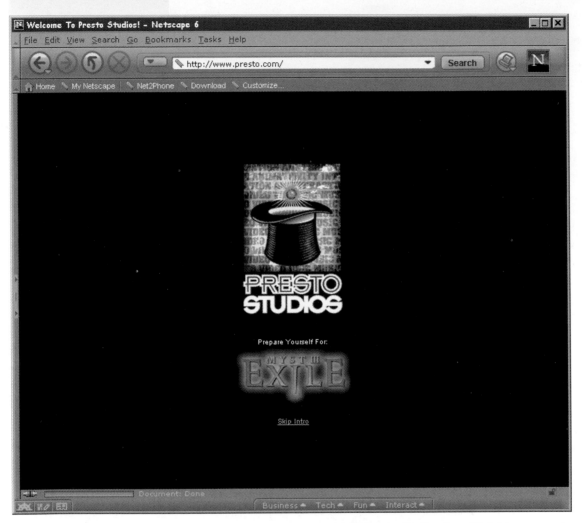

The interactive entertainment studio responsible for the design of such notable titles as the *Journeyman* series and the highly anticipated *Myst III: Exile*, Presto Studios's web site successfully combines bold colors, clean design, and simple navigation. Created by Joshua Scott, Presto Studios's IT Manager, the web site exemplifies excellent user-centered design.

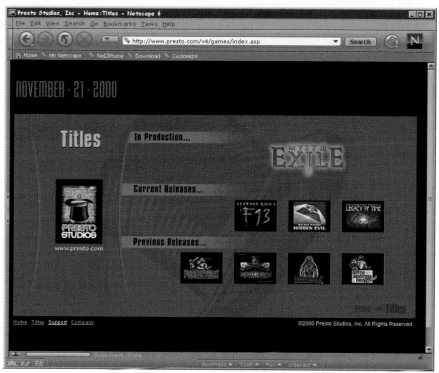

Presto Studios's web site was fashioned by creating a series of design templates in various vector formats that were then converted to GIFs and JPEGs and optimized with Fireworks.

The site uses bold and complementary colors in each of the various subsections to aid in navigation.

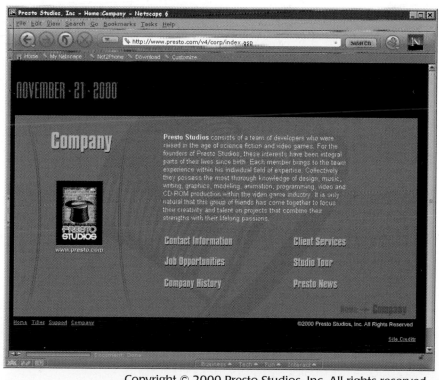

Braincraft

www.braincraft.com

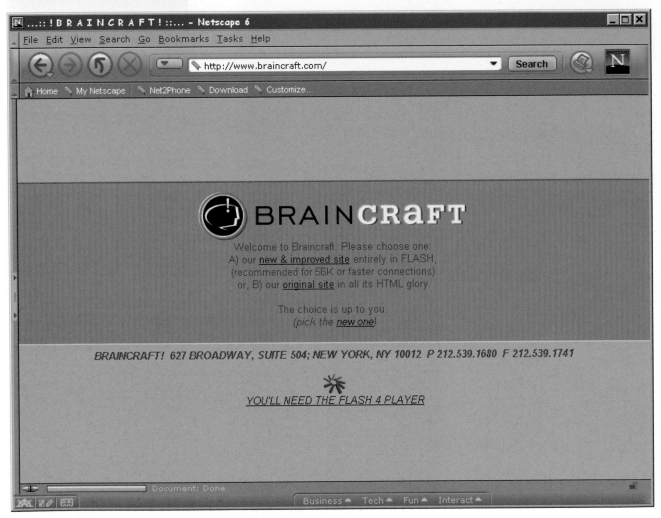

Founded in 1995 by President/CEO, Dan Stechow, and Executive VP/COO, Kevin Marth, Braincraft combines cutting-edge programming techniques, advanced instructional design methodologies, out-of-the-box design, and proven project management methods to offer dependable solutions for business-to-business customers.

Braincraft.com is an excellent example of cutting-edge and creative visual design. The beautiful and imminently usable interface, which was created using Macromedia Flash, is framed by a series of pop-up windows created and controlled by Dreamweaver HTML.

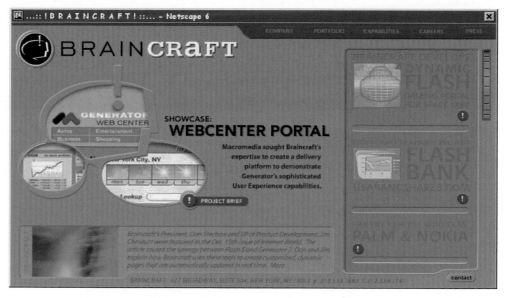

During the creation of their self-promotional site, Braincraft used Fireworks to compress hundreds of clean, professional, and fast-loading bitmaps for quick delivery over the web.

The Glenn A. Black
Laboratory of Archaeology

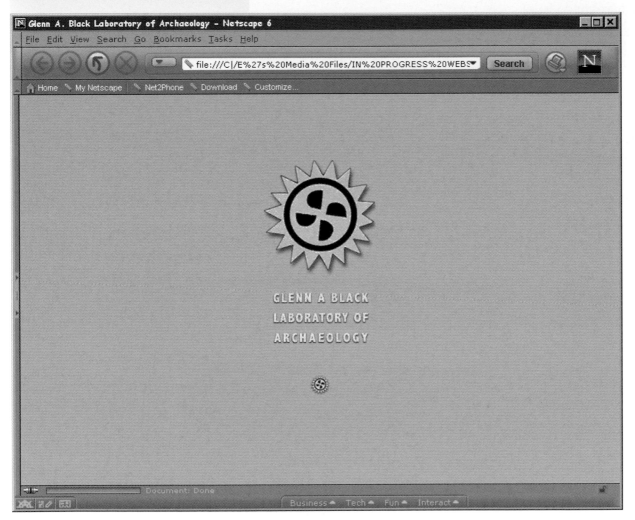

The Glenn Black Lab of Archaeology, an independent research unit on the campus of Indiana University, Bloomington, has always been dedicated to the use of information technology in the field of archaeology. The prototype v.2 update of the lab's web site, which is currently being developed by the author, will serve to publish the results of archaeological excavations, publicize the extensive activities of the lab, and act as a platform for future information technology projects.

The Glenn A. Black
Laboratory of Archaeology

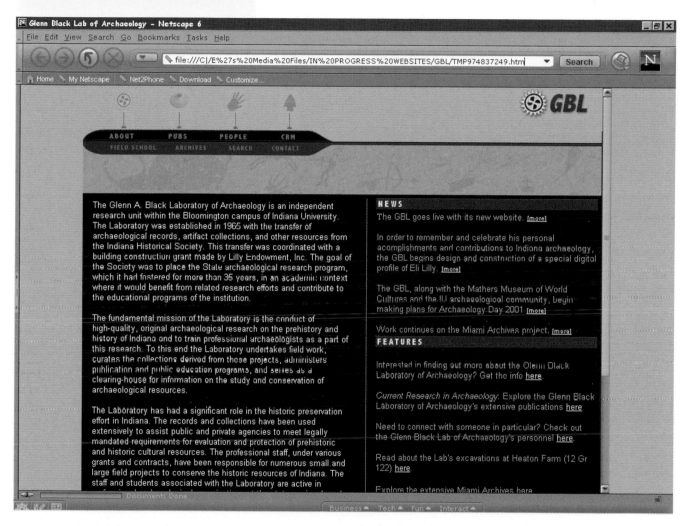

The Glenn Black Laboratory's web site uses an "earthy" palette of colors combined with archaeologically oriented design elements in order to visually reinforce its content. All the web site's original graphics were created and optimized using Fireworks.

The Glenn A. Black
Laboratory of Archaeology

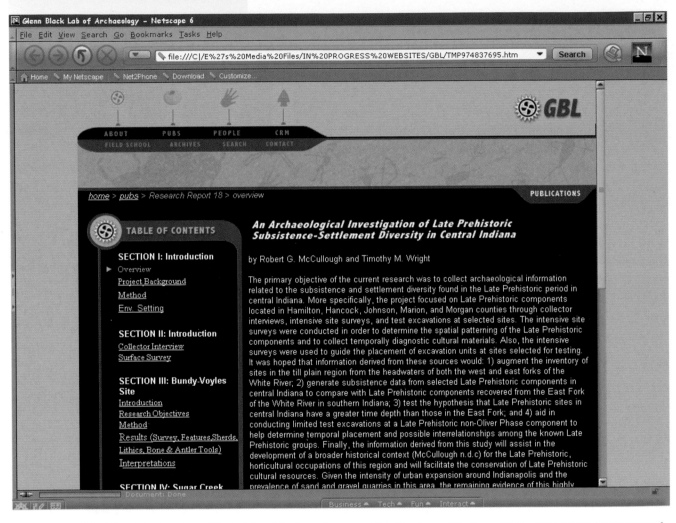

Laid out exclusively with tables in Dreamweaver, the web site balances appealing design and usability in order to maximize the delivery and accessibility of information.

3. Click the swatch to the right of the word "Custom" to open the Color Picker.

New Document

Canvas Size: 976.6K

Width: 500 | Pixels | W: 500
Height: 500 | Pixels | H: 500
Resolution: 72 | Pixels/Inch

Canvas Color:
- ○ White
- ○ Transparent
- ● Custom

[OK] [Cancel]

4. Move your cursor (which turns into an eyedropper when you open the Color Picker) over the desired color and click your mouse button once. You'll notice the swatch in the New Document dialog box changes into the chosen color.

New Document

Canvas Size: 976.6K

Width: 500 | Pixels | W: 500
Height: 500 | Pixels | H: 500
Resolution: 72 | Pixels/Inch

Canvas Color:
- ○ White
- ○ Transparent
- ● Custom

#C0C0C0

[Cancel]

5. Click OK.

Opening an Existing File

You will get to the point where you'll need to open a document that you've already been working on. To do this, follow these steps:

1. Go to File ➢ Open, or use the shortcut Cmd/Ctrl+O.

2. When the file navigation screen appears, locate and select the Fireworks file you want to open.

Tip

Firework's native file format is PNG, so if you have a PNG that was created with another graphics program, you can open that as well.

Opening Multiple Files

During the production of the various screenshots for this book, I found that it was really tedious to open one screenshot file, edit it, export it, close it, and then do the whole process again with the next one. Once I started taking advantage of Fireworks's ability to open multiple documents at one time, I could open all the files that I wanted to edit, and then would have one less thing to worry about as I was working. You can take advantage of this snazzy feature by following these steps:

1. Go to File ➢ Open, or use the shortcut Cmd/Ctrl+O.

2. When the file navigation screen appears, locate and select the first Fireworks file you want to open.

3. Then, with the Cmd/Ctrl key held down, select any additional files you want to open.

4. When you've selected all the files you want to open, click the Open button in the file navigation screen.

When you open multiple files in Fireworks, they appear one on top of the other (with the most recent on the top). To move between them, simply click the Document Window of the image with which you want to work.

Opening Other Image File Types

You certainly aren't limited to just opening the PNG files in Fireworks. The program wouldn't be as useful if you couldn't open the wide range of graphic files created in other applications. The process for opening other file types in Fireworks is almost identical to opening a PNG. There are, however, a few minor differences that are important.

Tip

Fireworks can open PICT (Macintosh) files, Macromedia FreeHand files (FH7, FH8), Adobe Illustrator files (AI7, AI8), EPS files, layered Photoshop files (PSD), CorelDRAW 8 files, GIFs, JPEGs, BMPs, TIFFs, PNGs (Windows and Macintosh), WBMP files, TGA, ASCII text, and RTF text.

To open a file type other than a PNG, follow these steps:

1. Go to File ➤ Open, or use the shortcut Cmd/Ctrl+O.

2. When the file navigation screen appears, use the Files of Type drop-down menu to select the type of file you want to open.

3. Locate and select the file you want to open.

Note

If you've already created a new document in Fireworks, you'll notice that there is an Import command in the File menu. What's the difference between Import and Open? The Open command simply opens the desired file (whether a PNG or some other type) as a new document. The Import command reads the desired file and places its contents in an existing document.

Summary

This chapter looked at the ways to set the stage for the creation of a new image. It explored the steps you need to take to create a new document. It also looked at opening an existing document, opening multiple documents at the same time, and opening a non-Fireworks (PNG) file.

Part 5

Creating Content in Fireworks

Up to this point, we've looked at how to work with the interface, open existing documents, and create new documents. In this part of the book, we're going to explore the tools and techniques for creating actual graphics in Fireworks. We'll start off by creating and editing bitmaps and vector images, and then we'll work with stroke and fill. Finally, we'll look at how to create and edit text in Fireworks.

Creating Content in Fireworks

Chapter 9

Creating and Manipulating Images

Now that you've learned how to get around in Fireworks, you'll learn to use the tools that will empower you to set your inner Michelangelo free (or Matt Groening for that matter). Images make the web go around (so to speak), so it's time to start creating!

In this chapter, you'll explore the tools and techniques in Fireworks that will let you create your own images. There are some tools, however, that—because this book is designed to be an introduction to Dreamweaver and Fireworks—we aren't able to cover. If you are interested in the advanced aspects of any of the Fireworks image-creation and manipulation tools, you should check on the program's Help function or check out *Mastering Dreamweaver 4 and Fireworks 4* by David Crowder and Rhonda Crowder (Sybex, 2001). Topics in this chapter include:

- Working with layers
- Understanding bitmaps
- Working with bitmap images in Bitmap Edit Mode
- Understanding vectors
- Creating basic shapes, free-form paths, and lines
- Applying stroke
- Applying fill

Working with Layers

It's very important to get a handle on using the Layers panel early on in your exposure to Fireworks's image-creation and manipulation tools.

Note

If you're having trouble remembering exactly what layers are, flip back to Chapter 7, "Before You Get Started with Fireworks," and take a look at the section that discusses the Layers panel.

With the Layers panel, you can add, delete, and edit layers in your current document with the simple click of a few buttons. To access the Layers panel, go to Windows ➢ Layers, or use the shortcut F2.

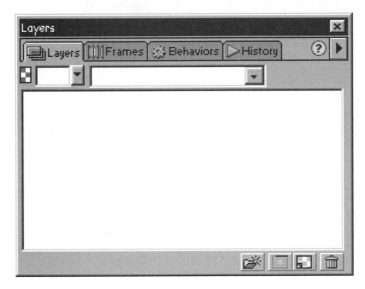

If you don't have a fresh Document Window open, create a new document and see what happens in the Layers panel. You'll notice that Fireworks automatically creates a layer (called Layer 1 by default).

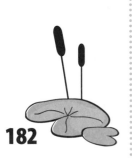

Thumbnail Images

Whenever you add an element (line, text, rectangle, etc.) to a layer, Fireworks creates a thumbnail image of that element in a sublayer. You can select that specific element by clicking its thumbnail. To hide the thumbnails, click the − (minus sign) icon to the left of the layer. Conversely, if you want to view the thumbnails (after having collapsed the layer), click the + (plus sign) icon.

There is another layer in the Layers panel called the Web Layer.

The Web Layer is a special layer that appears initially as the top layer in each new document, and contains web objects, such as hotspots and slices, used for assigning interactivity to exported Fireworks documents. You cannot delete, duplicate, move, or rename the Web Layer.

Note

To find more information on the Web Layer, hotspots, or slices in Fireworks, see *Mastering Dreamweaver 4 and Fireworks 4* by David Crowder and Rhonda Crowder (Sybex, 2001).

Adding a Layer

You certainly aren't stuck with the one layer that is created when you open a new document. One of the joys of layers is that you can create as many as you desire.

To add a new layer using the Layers panel, follow these steps:

1. If you don't already have the Layers panel open, select Windows ➢ Layers, or use the shortcut F2.

2. Click the small right-pointing arrow in the upper-right corner of the Layers panel to open the Options pop-up menu.

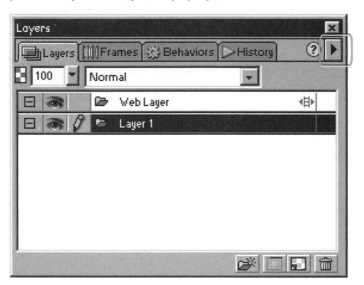

3. Choose New Layer.

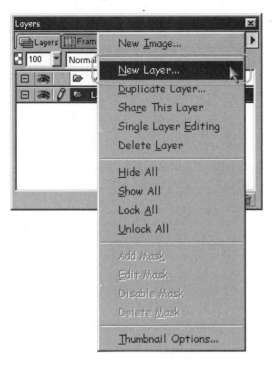

4. When the New Layer dialog box pops up, type the name of your layer in the Name field.

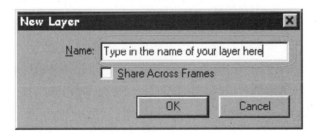

5. Click OK.

There are two other ways to insert a new layer. First, you can click the New/Duplicate Layer button in the bottom-right corner of the Layers panel.

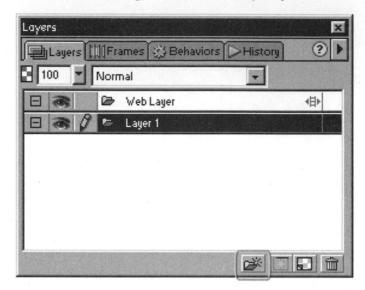

Alternatively, you can add a new layer to your current document by selecting Insert ➢ Layer. A blank layer is then inserted before the current layer. The new layer becomes the active layer and is highlighted in the Layers panel.

Deleting a Layer

You can just as easily delete a layer as you can add one.

Warning

Remember that when you delete a layer, you also delete all content on that layer.

The first, and most common, way to delete a layer goes something like this:

1. If you don't already have the Layers panel open, select Windows ➢ Layers, or use the shortcut F2.

2. Select the layer you want to delete by clicking it in the Layers panel.

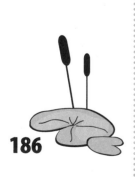

3. Click the small right-pointing arrow in the upper-right corner of the Layers panel to open the Options pop-up menu.

4. Choose Delete Layer from the Options pop-up menu.

Warning

Be absolutely sure you've selected the correct layer, as Fireworks doesn't prompt you for confirmation of your action.

Alternatively, you can delete a layer by first selecting it in the Layers panel and then clicking the Delete Selection button.

Turning Layer Visibility On and Off

One of the great things about layers is that they can be "turned off." When you do this, those layers become invisible. Ultimately, this helps to unclutter your current working image and allows you to better focus on a particular section in a particular layer. After, you simply turn the layer back on.

To turn the visibility of a layer on or off, follow these steps:

1. If you don't already have the Layers panel open, select Windows ➢ Layers, or use the shortcut F2.

2. Select the layer whose visibility you want to turn on or off.

3. Click the eye icon just to the left of the layer. If the eye is not visible, the layer is currently "off." If the eye is open, the current layer is "on."

Understanding Bitmaps

Generally speaking, there are two groups of graphic file types out there: **bitmaps** and **vectors**. All of the image file types we've already talked about (GIFs, JPEGs, and PNGs) are bitmaps. Bitmaps, which are also called raster graphics, are images that are composed of individual pixels that are a fixed size and take up a set amount of computer memory. The quality of a bitmap image is determined by its resolution. A bitmap with a higher resolution (say, 300 dpi) will be better quality than one with a lower resolution (say, 72 dpi). Another characteristic of a bitmap image is that it is resolution dependent. When the resolution of a bitmap is set, it is fixed. One of the most poignant examples of this is something called "jaggies." If you take a bitmap image and either zoom in or enlarge it, you'll be able to see its individual pixels. The edges of the image will have a jaggy appearance because the number of pixels per inch cannot change.

Bitmaps

Bitmaps are images that are composed of individual pixels that are a fixed size and take up a set amount of computer memory.

Vectors

Vector images are made up of lines, curves, and points that form shapes through a set of mathematical instructions.

Starting Bitmap Edit Mode

Even though the majority of the images you create in Fireworks are ultimately destined for export in a bitmap form (GIF, JPEG, PNG), the main image-creation and manipulation tools you'll use are geared toward vectors. The tools designed specifically for working with bitmaps are geared less toward creation and more toward editing. Fireworks, therefore, has two primary modes: Bitmap Edit Mode and Vector Edit Mode. If you open a bitmap image or use any of the tools described below, Fireworks automatically switches from Vector Edit Mode (which is the default) to Bitmap Edit Mode. When you're in Bitmap Edit Mode, Fireworks will tell you by displaying the words "Bitmap Mode" in the title bar of your Document Window.

Fireworks also displays a striped border around your Document Window when you're in Bitmap Edit Mode.

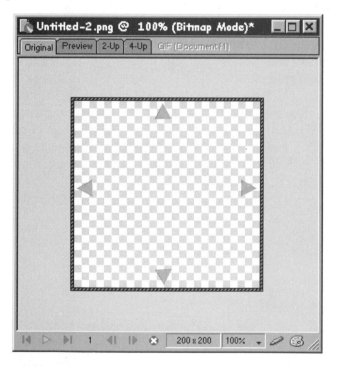

The Limits of Bitmap Edit Mode

In all honesty, Bitmap Edit Mode is pretty limiting. Some tools don't work in Bitmap Edit Mode, while others work far better in Vector Edit Mode. For example, if you were to draw a line across a bitmap with the Pencil tool in Bitmap Edit Mode, that line would become a permanent part of the bitmap. On the other hand, if you did the same thing in Vector Edit Mode (something we'll talk about later in this chapter), you would create a vector that could be moved, changed, or deleted.

Here's a list of the of ways to enter Bitmap Edit Mode:

◇ When you open a bitmap image in Fireworks, you are automatically switched to Bitmap Edit Mode. (Remember to look for the words "Bitmap Mode" in the title bar or the striped border around the entire Document Window to indicate Bitmap Edit Mode.)

◇ Select a bitmap image from the Layers panel.

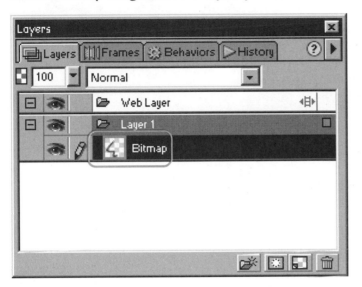

◇ Select the bitmap with the Pointer tool in the Toolbox and then go to Modify ➢ Edit Bitmap, or use the shortcut Command+E (Macintosh) or Ctrl+E (Windows).

Tip

If you are having trouble selecting the bitmap image with the Pointer tool, hold down your mouse button and move your cursor over the image. When you release your cursor, the bitmap image will be selected.

- Select a bitmap image with any of these tools (all of which we'll talk about in the next section of this chapter): Marquee, Ellipse Marquee, Lasso, Polygon Lasso, or Magic Wand.

Closing Bitmap Edit Mode

As is the case when entering Bitmap Edit Mode, there are a number of ways to exit Bitmap Edit Mode:

- Select a vector object from the Layers panel.

Layers

Layers | Frames | Behaviors | History

100 | Normal

Web Layer

Layer 1

Path

Bitmap

◇ Double-click your mouse in an area outside the bitmap image with the Pointer, the Subselection Pointer, or the Lasso.

Tools

Colors

View

◇ Click the Stop button located at the bottom of the Document Window.

Untitled-2.png @ 100% (Bitm...

| Original | Preview | 2-Up | 4-Up | GIF (Document A) |

200 x 200   100%

◇ Go to Modify ➤ Exit Bitmap Mode or use the shortcut Cmd+Option+E (Mac) or Ctrl+Shift+E (Win).

◇ Press Esc.

Working with Bitmap Edit Mode Tools

There are several tools that are native to Bitmap Edit Mode. When you use these tools while in the default Vector Edit Mode, you are automatically switched over to Bitmap Edit Mode. For editing purposes, these tools are pretty much restricted to selection tools, such as the Marquee tool, the Lasso, and the Magic Wand. You also have access to the Eraser and the Crop tool.

For More Information

There are other, more advanced Bitmap Edit Mode tools that fall beyond the scope of this book. They include the Cloning tool, the Bitmap Paint tool, and the Bitmap Transformation tool. For further information on these tools, check out the Fireworks Help function (Help, Using Fireworks) or refer to Mastering Dreamweaver 4 and Fireworks 4 by David Crowder and Rhonda Crowder (Sybex, 2001).

Tip

If you double-click any of the following tools in the Toolbox, Fireworks automatically opens the Options panel. Use the panel to set your options (such as edge properties or selection tolerance).

Selecting a Rectangular Area with the Marquee Tool

The Rectangular Marquee tool is used to select a rectangular area of a bitmap image. (The Marquee tool itself is one of those tool groups mentioned in Chapter 7.)

Tip

The Marquee tool group also contains the Marquee tool and the Elliptical Marquee tool.

To use this tool, follow these steps:

1. Select the Rectangular Marquee tool from the Toolbox with a single mouse click.

2. Move your mouse over the section of the bitmap image you want to select.

3. Hold down the mouse button and drag the pointer over the area you want to select.

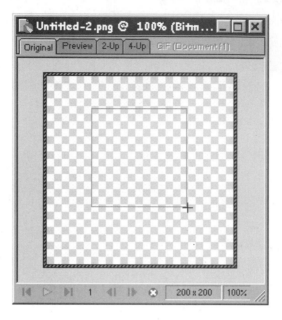

4. When you are satisfied with your selection, release the mouse button. Notice that the area is highlighted by a moving dotted line.

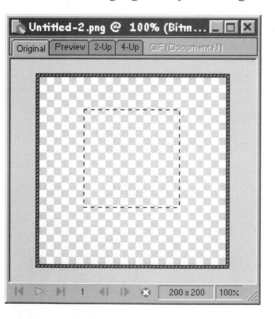

Selecting an Elliptical Area with the Marquee Tool

The Marquee tool group also contains the Elliptical Marquee tool. While the Rectangular Marquee tool selected an area that was, obviously, rectangular, the Elliptical Marquee tool selects an area that is an oval or circle. To use it, follow these steps:

1. Select the Elliptical Marquee tool from the Toolbox.

2. Move your mouse over the section of the bitmap image you want to select.

3. Hold down the mouse button and drag the pointer over the area you want to select.

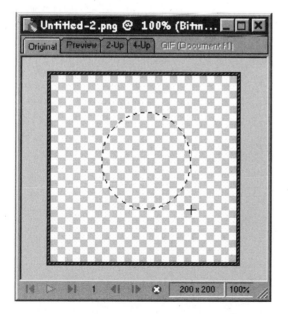

197

4. When you are satisfied with your selection, release the mouse button. Notice that the area is highlighted by a moving dotted line.

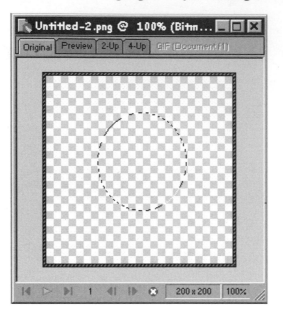

 Tip

If you hold down Shift while using any of the tools in the Marquee tool group, you'll "draw" a perfectly proportioned square or circle. On the other hand, if you hold down the Opt/Alt key while using any of the tools in the Marquee tool group, your shape will "draw" from the center of the shape rather than from the corner.

Using the Lasso Tool to Select an Irregular Area

The Marquee tool is great for selecting a regular area, but what if you need to select an irregular area? The Lasso tool allows you to draw an irregular or free-form selection area. To try it out, follow these steps:

1. Select the Lasso tool from the Toolbox.

2. Move the cursor (which has turned into the Lasso icon) to the area where you want to start drawing your selection.

3. With your mouse button depressed, draw the area that you want to select. Notice that as you do, the selection line drawn by the Lasso tool is pale blue.

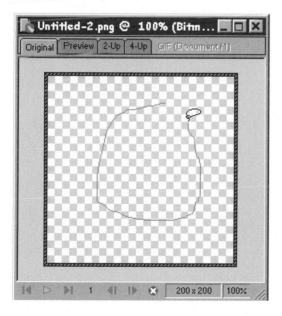

4. When you finish drawing the area you want to select (which should be back where you began), a small black box appears to the bottom right of the Lasso icon. This signals that you have successfully selected a "closed" area.

5. Release your mouse button. Notice that the area you selected is highlighted by a moving dotted line.

Tip

The second tool in the Lasso tool group is the Polygon Lasso. Try it out; it works the same as Dreamweaver's Polygon Hotspot tool that we discussed in Chapter 5, "Working with Hyperlinks."

Using the Magic Wand

So far, the tools we've discussed have selected a given section of your bitmap image based on an area that you define. The Magic Wand, however, selects an area based on similar color. Let's try it out:

1. Double-click the Magic Wand tool in the Toolbox.

2. Once the Options panel opens, set the tolerance level by entering a value into the Tolerance field. (When you set the tolerance, you're setting a range of colors that is included in the Magic Wand's selection. A higher tolerance will mean that a wider range of associated colors will be selected. A lower tolerance means that fewer associated colors will be included in the selection.)

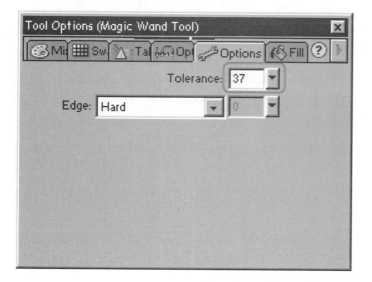

3. Click an area of color you want to select in your bitmap image. You'll notice that the moving dashed border highlights your selection area.

Erasing with the Eraser

The Eraser tool is used either to remove pixels from your bitmap image or to color over pixels with a different color.

Eraser Options

When you initially select the Eraser tool, it has a default size and edge characteristic. You can easily change the size, shape (from circular to square), edge effect, and Set to Erase Color options with the various sliders and pop-up menus in the Eraser Options panel (which is accessed by double-clicking the Eraser tool in the Toolbox). The Set to Erase Color option dictates exactly how your erased area will look (filled with another color vs. removed totally). Fill color and stroke color will be discussed later in this chapter.

Follow this process to erase:

1. Select the Eraser tool in the Toolbox.

2. Move the cursor over the area you want to erase.

3. Hold down your mouse button and move the cursor over the areas you want erased. Depending on your Set to Erase Color settings, you'll see the effect immediately.

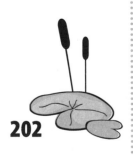

Cropping in Bitmap Edit Mode

The final tool we're going to look at in this section is the Crop tool. Basically, the Crop tool is used to remove portions of an image. Let's take a look at how it works:

1. Select the Crop tool from the Toolbox.

2. Hold down the mouse button and drag the cursor over the area you want to select.

3. Release the mouse button when you are satisfied with the selected area.

If you aren't perfectly satisfied with the selected area, adjust the bounding box by dragging the handles.

4. With the Crop tool still selected, double-click within the selected area (or press Enter) to crop the image. Remember that everything *outside* the selected area will be removed.

Warning

If you click another tool in the Toolbox before cropping the image, the crop selection area will disappear and you'll have to go through these steps again.

Understanding Vector Images

Unlike bitmaps, which are composed of pixels, vector images are made up of lines, curves, and points that form shapes through a set of mathematical instructions. Because of the mathematical instructions that make up a vector image, they can be enlarged or shrunk while maintaining the same quality. For example, when you enlarge a vector image, the program recalculates the dimensions of the image. As a result, vector images will look smooth and crisp at any resolution. (If you try these adjustments with a bitmap, you get the horrible "jaggies" we talked about earlier in this chapter.)

Tip

Vector images generally work better for line art and detailed illustration. They don't work well for continuous color or photorealistic images.

As mentioned before, most of the Fireworks tools are intended for the creation and manipulation of vector images. The downside to this is that the web can't natively display vector images. As a result, all of your vector art in Fireworks is transformed into a bitmap image (GIF, JPEG, or PNG) when it is exported. The upside is that you can create a heck of a lot more with the vector tools in Fireworks than with the bitmap tools.

Note

Macromedia Flash uses vector images, but a plug-in is needed to view them over the web.

Working in Vector Edit Mode

Vector Edit Mode is the default mode in Fireworks. So, unless you explicitly enter Bitmap Edit Mode, you'll always be in Vector Edit Mode. You'll immediately find that Vector Edit Mode is where you'll do the majority of your creative work in Fireworks, because it gives access to the kind of drawing tools that will set your creativity free.

Creating Basic Shapes

Most images (whether a button destined for inclusion in a web page or a complex corporate logo) are made up of basic shapes. Fireworks offers some easy-to-use tools that allow you to create and edit basic shapes without having to draw them freehand.

Drawing a Rectangle or Square

To draw a rectangle or square, follow these steps:

1. Choose the Rectangle tool from the Toolbox.

Tip

The tools for creating basics shapes are all in one tool group.

2. Move your cursor (which has become a crosshair) to the location in your document where you want to start the rectangle.

3. Click your mouse button and drag the outline of the rectangle until It is exactly how you want It. Notice that the rectangle is outlined in blue as you are dragging it.

Tip

Hold down Shift at the same time as you click and drag to draw a perfectly proportioned square.

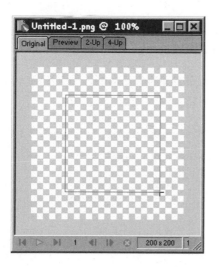

4. When the shape and size are exactly how you want them, release your mouse button.

Note

You'll notice that your rectangle is solid white, but what if you want your shape to be another color? If you're itching to learn how to change the color of your shape, jump forward to the section in this chapter titled "Applying Fill with the Fill Panel."

Drawing a Rounded Rectangle

The rectangle that we've just finished drawing has corners that are at right angles. Luckily, Fireworks also has a tool designed specifically for creating rectangles with rounded corners. Let's take a look at how to use this tool:

1. Choose the Rounded Rectangle tool from the Toolbox.

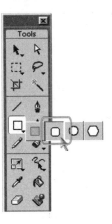

2. Move your cursor (which has become a crosshair) to the location in your document where you want to start the rectangle.

3. Click your mouse button and drag the outline of the rounded rectangle until it is exactly how you want it.

4. With the mouse button still held down, either press the Up key to increase the roundness of your corners or the Down key to decrease their roundness.

5. Release the mouse button when the roundness is set.

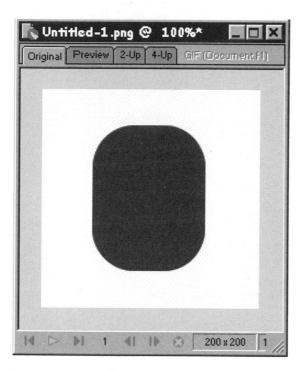

You can change the corner roundness of a rectangle you've already created by using the Object panel in the following way:

1. With the Pointer tool, select the rounded rectangle with which you want to work.

2. Go to Window ➢ Object, or use the shortcut Opt/Alt+F2, to open the Object panel.

3. To change the roundness of the rectangle's corners, simply enter a new value in the Roundness field.

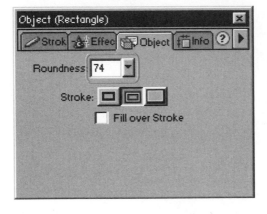

Alternatively, you can adjust the Roundness slider by clicking the small right-pointing arrow next to the Roundness field.

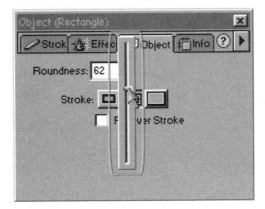

Drawing an Ellipse or Circle

To draw an ellipse or a circle, follow these steps:

1. Select the Ellipse tool from the Toolbox.

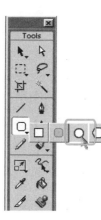

2. Move your cursor (which has become a crosshair) to the location in your document where you want to start the ellipse.

3. Click your mouse button and drag the outline of the ellipse until it is exactly how you want it.

Tip

To create a perfect circle, hold down Shift while you draw the ellipse.

4. Release the mouse button once the ellipse is the shape and size you want it.

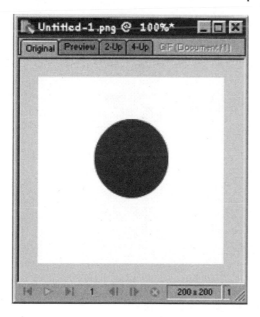

Drawing a Polygon

To use the Polygon tool, you need to do a couple of things before you actually draw the polygon in your document. Let's take a look:

1. Double click the Polygon tool in the Toolbox to open the Polygon tool Options panel.

2. Choose Polygon from the Shape pop-up menu.

3. Enter the number of desired sides for the polygon in the Sides field.

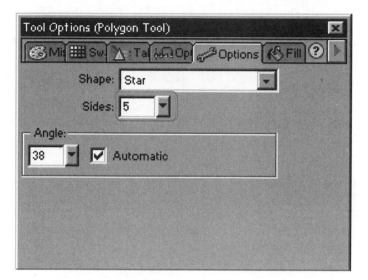

4. Move your cursor (which has become a crosshair) to the location in your document where you want to start the polygon.

5. Click your mouse button and drag the outline of the polygon until it is exactly how you want it.

6. Release the mouse button.

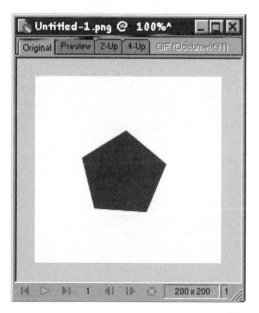

Drawing a Star

Drawing a star is almost the same as drawing a polygon:

1. Double-click the Polygon tool in the Toolbox to open the Polygon tool Options panel.

2. Choose Star from the Shape pop-up menu.

3. Enter the number of sides (points) in the Sides field.

4. Enter the angle of the sides (points) in the Angle field.

Tool Options (Polygon Tool)

Shape: Star

Sides: 5

Angle: 38 ☑ Automatic

Tip

The lower the angle, the pointier your star will be.

5. Move your cursor (which has become a crosshair) to the location in your document where you want to start drawing the star.

6. Click your mouse button and drag the outline of the star until it is exactly how you want it.

7. Release the mouse button.

Creating Free-Form Paths and Lines

When you draw a squiggly line with the Pencil tool, for example, Fireworks creates a shape that is made up of two things: points and paths.

Imagine that the line you drew with the Pencil tool is a connect-the-dots drawing. The points are the dots you connect. In the same example, paths are simply the lines and curves that connect the points. In this section, you'll look at three tools you can use to make free-form paths and lines: the Line tool, the Pencil tool, and the Brush tool.

Note

There are several advanced tools used to create free-form lines and paths, most notably the Pen tool. For more information on the Pen tool, which can get pretty complicated, see the Fireworks Help function.

Point
The manipulatable dots which, along with paths, make up a vector shape.

Path
With vector graphics, paths are the lines or curves that connect points to make a shape.

Drawing a Straight Line

As its name implies, the Line tool draws a straight line. Let's look at how:

1. Select the Line tool from the Toolbox.

2. Move your cursor (which has become a crosshair) to the location in your document where you want to start the line.

3. Hold down the mouse button and drag the cursor to where you want the line to end.

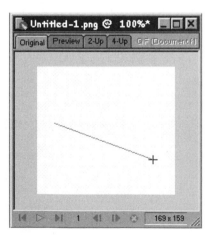

4. When the line is the length you want, release the mouse button. Voila! A straight line!

Notice that, until you select another object (line, shape, etc.), the line you've just drawn is blue. This just means that it's a path. Simply click anywhere off the line with the Selection tool, and the line reverts back to its default stroke color.

Note

You aren't stuck with the default black line when you initially draw it. If you are itching to change how the line looks, flip forward to the section in this chapter titled "Applying Stroke with the Stroke Panel."

Drawing a Free-Form Path with the Pencil Tool

A straight line is fine and good, but what if you want to draw a freeform path? This is where the free-form path tools come in. Let's take a look at how one of these tools, the Pencil tool, works:

1. Choose the Pencil tool from the Toolbox.

2. Move your cursor (which has become a pencil icon) to the location in your document where you want to start the path.

3. Hold down the mouse button and draw the free-form path you want.

4. Once your free-form path is exactly how you want it, release the mouse button.

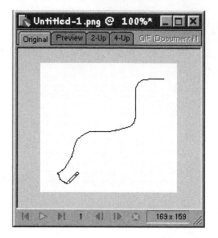

Notice that when you release the mouse button, your line is blue and composed of a bunch of dots. These dots are the points that make up the path. To see what your free-form path actually looks like (without the points), just click anywhere off of it with the Selection tool.

Drawing a Free-Form Path with the Brush Tool

Unlike the Pencil tool, which by default draws a free-form path with a 1-pixel width, the Brush tool draws a free-form path that is much thicker and, true to its name, looks more like a brush stroke.

 Note

The way that the free-form path drawn by both the Pencil tool and the Brush tool looks is infinitely changeable with the Stroke panel.

Let's take a look at how the Brush tool works:

1. Select the Brush tool from the Toolbox.

2. Move your cursor (which has become an empty circle icon) to the location in your document where you want to start the path.

3. Hold down the mouse button and draw the free-form path you want.

4. Once your free-form path is exactly how you want it, release the mouse button.

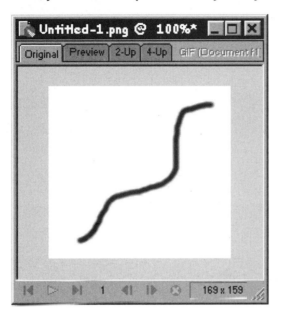

Using the Subselection Tool to Edit Points

Points play an important role in the vector objects you've created. It's no exaggeration to say that these points—those little blue dots that make up a square, an ellipse, a star, or a free-form path—are the heart of a vector object. They give you the ability to alter an object by changing the location of individual points. When a point is moved, the rest of the shape (whether a rectangle or free-form path) changes accordingly.

Use the Subselection tool to edit points in a star:

1. If you don't already have a star in your document, insert one by using the Polygon tool in the Toolbox.

2. Select the Subselection tool (which is represented by a white arrow) from the Toolbox.

3. With the Subselection tool, select the star in your document. You'll notice that the points in the star, which were previously solid blue, become white with a blue border.

4. Click one of the points.

5. With the mouse button held down, drag the point to a new position.

6. When you reach the position where you want to move the point, release your mouse button. Notice how the path redraws itself to accommodate the point's new position.

Note

Although we used a star in this example, it's important to note that the process works the same on any other vector object.

Applying Stroke with the Stroke Panel

Stroke is the character of the line formed when you draw a vector object. Thickness, color, and texture are all part of stroke. Whether you want to change the character of a line drawn with the Pencil tool or of the border of a rounded rectangle, learning Fireworks's stroke tools is an important step of your journey in the land of Macromedia.

The primary tool used to change and manipulate the stroke of an object is the Stroke panel. With it, you have total control over every tool nuance, including ink amount, tip size and shape, texture, and edge effect. Also, sensitivity settings control how a pressure-sensitive pen affects strokes. This section will walk through the various changes you can make to the stroke of an object.

Applying Stroke with the Pencil Tool

You can start this exercise with a document whose background is a color rather than white or transparent, so that the rectangle stands out better.

1. Draw a rectangle using the Rectangle tool. (Flip back to the section of this chapter titled "Drawing a Rectangle or Square" if you need help.)

Note

You can start this exercise with a document whose background is a color, rather than white or transparent, so that the rectangle stands out better. If you forget how to do this, flip back to Chapter 7 to refresh your memory. You can also change the background color by going to Modify ➢ Canvas Color.

2. Select the rectangle, which is currently solid white, with the Selection tool in the Toolbox.

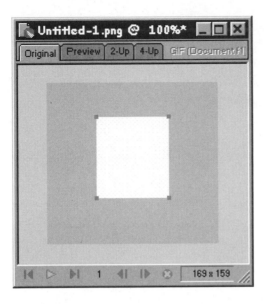

At this point, the stroke of the rectangle isn't visible, but it's there. It's just hidden at the moment.

3. If you don't already have the Stroke panel open, go to Window ➢ Stroke, or use the shortcut Cmd+Opt+F4/Ctrl+Alt+F4.

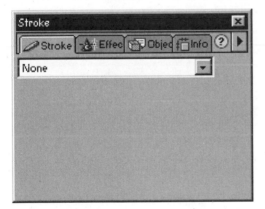

4. Make sure the rectangle is selected. (The Stroke panel is empty, because "None" has been automatically selected from the Stroke Category pop-up menu.)

5. Select a stroke category (other than None) from the Stroke Category pop-up menu. For our purposes, we'll choose Pencil.

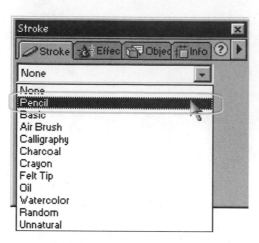

Note

We've just chosen one out of eleven possible choices in the Stroke Category menu. Try selecting the others, and you'll see that they each have a distinct look.

After choosing Pencil from the Stroke Category pop-up menu, you'll notice that two things happen. First, the remainder of the Stroke panel becomes active.

Second, the rectangle has acquired a thin black border. This black border is the stroke.

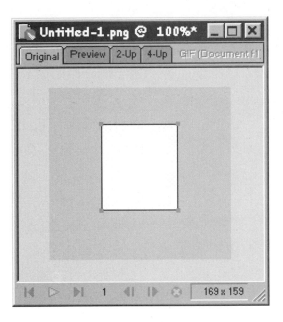

Changing the Stroke Color

You can now make various changes to the parameters of the Pencil Stroke Category. The first changes the color of the stroke:

1. With the Stroke panel open and the rectangle selected, click the color swatch (which should currently be black) to open the Color Palette.

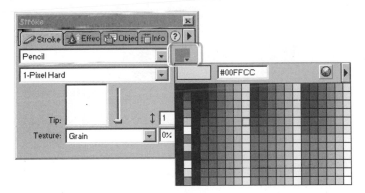

2. With the Color Palette open, move your cursor (which is now in the form of an eyedropper icon) over the color you desire and click your mouse button. You'll notice that the stroke automatically changes color.

If you aren't happy with the colors available, you can mix your own color in the Color dialog box:

1. With the Color Palette open, click the Open Color Dialog box button.

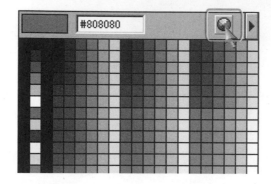

2. The Color dialog box opens.

From here, you can choose the specific color you want by entering a numeric RGB code.

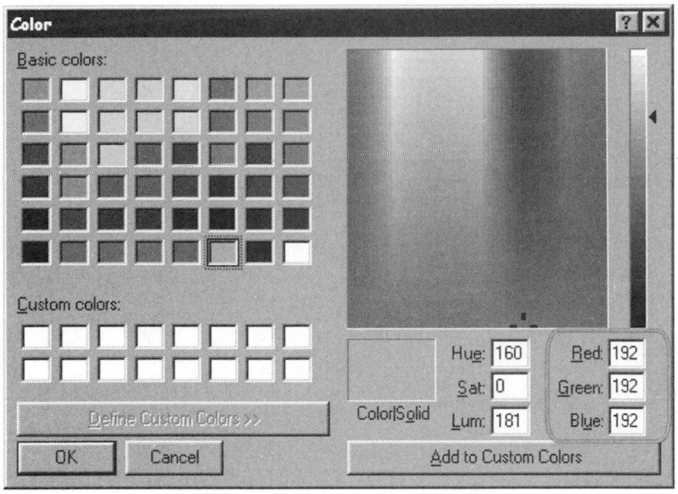

Or you can enter Hue, Sat, and Lum values.

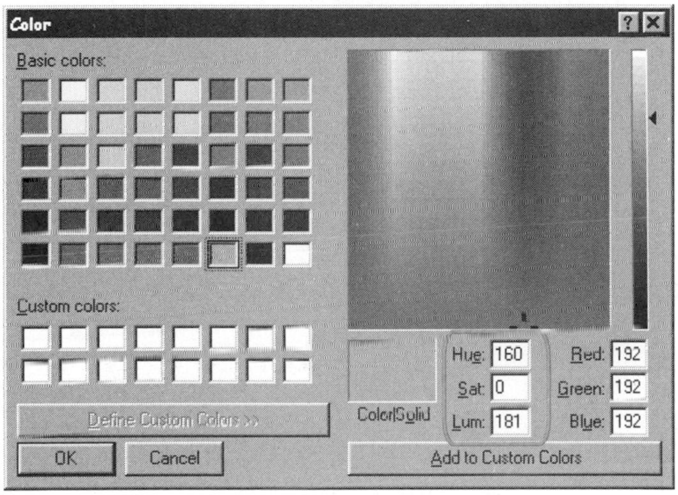

Or you can set the shade with the Shade slider.

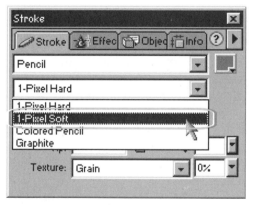

Setting the Stroke Name

Follow these steps to set the stroke name:

1. Make sure that the Stroke panel is open and the rectangle is selected.

2. Choose an option from the Stroke Name drop-down menu. For our purposes, we'll select 1-Pixel Soft.

> **Note**
>
> The individual stroke names vary between stroke categories. Experiment with various combinations to see what results you can get.

Changing the Stroke's Tip Size and Edge Softness

You'll notice that when you change the stroke name to 1-Pixel Soft, there isn't much of a visible change. This is because the size of the tip (the width of the stroke) isn't substantial. When we increase the tip size and change the edge softness in this section, you'll be able to see these changes far better. When you change the tip size, you either increase or decrease the dimensions of the tip. When you change the edge softness, you make the tip appear sharper or fuzzier.

Tip

When dealing with the tip characteristics, it's good to think of the stroke as being made with a real drawing tool (a brush, a pencil, etc.) so that when you change the tip characteristics, you are dynamically changing the type of tip the tool had when the stroke was drawn.

1. Make sure the Stroke panel is open and the rectangle is selected.

2. To change the edge softness, move the Tip Edge Softness slider up for fuzzier or down for sharper. You'll notice that the graphical representation of the tip will respond to reflect the changes you've made. For our purposes, maximize the tip softness by pushing the slider all the way to the top.

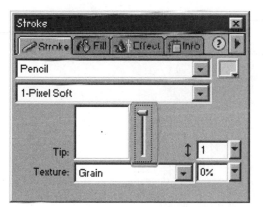

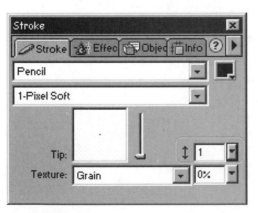

Maxing out the tip's fuzziness doesn't produce much of a visible change until you change the size of the tip itself.

3. To change the tip size, make sure the rectangle is still selected and the Stroke panel is open.

4. To increase the size of the tip, simply type a value in the Tip Size field. For our purposes, type in **25**.

Alternatively, you can use the Tip Size slider, which is accessed by clicking the small down-pointing arrow to the right of the Tip Size field. (Move the slider up to increase the size and down to decrease it.) Notice that the graphical representation of the tip changes to reflect the changes you've made.

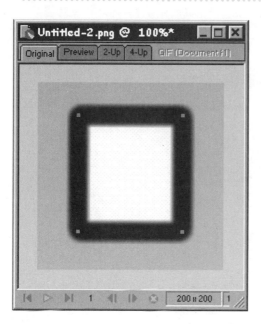

Setting the Stroke's Texture

When you set the texture of a stroke, you can actually determine a pattern that the stroke displays. Let's take a look at how it works:

1. Make sure the Stroke panel is open and the rectangle is selected.

2. Choose a texture from the Texture drop-down menu. You'll notice that a small preview pops up adjacent to each of the textures when you move your mouse over it.

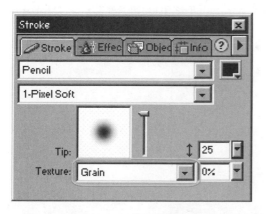

Choose Fiber from the drop-down menu. You'll notice that the rectangle's stroke texture automatically changes.

You can also set the amount of texture (by percent).

1. Make sure the Stroke panel is open and the rectangle is selected.

2. Type a value in the Amount of Texture field and hit Enter. For our purposes, type in **100%.**

   You can also adjust the amount of texture manually by using the slider, which is accessible by clicking the small down-pointing arrow just to the right of the field. The more texture you want visible, the higher the percent should be.

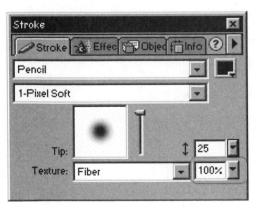

Applying Fill with the Fill Panel

Basically, fill is just the opposite of stroke. Instead of being the visual character of an object's edge or line, fill is the visual character of the inside of the object.

Note

Although we're only using a solid fill with the Fill panel here, Fireworks also allows you to fill an object with a gradient or a pattern. For more info on using gradients or patterns as fill, just check out Fireworks's Help function (Help ➢ Using Fireworks).

As you would expect, fill really only works on objects that have an "inside." Applying a fill to a free-form path wouldn't be of any use, as the line doesn't have an inside *to* fill.

Applying a Solid Fill

Let's dive right in and learn how to apply and manipulate a solid fill. Because we used a rectangle when discussing a stroke, we're going to work with an ellipse instead.

1. Draw an ellipse using the Ellipse tool. (If you don't remember exactly what you need to do to draw an ellipse, flip back to the section in this chapter titled "Drawing an Ellipse or Circle.")

2. Select the ellipse, which is currently solid white, with the Selection tool from the Toolbox.

Warning

If your document has a white background (as opposed to transparent or a different color), the ellipse itself won't be visible unless it is selected.

Fill

The visual character of the inside of an object, such as color, texture, etc.

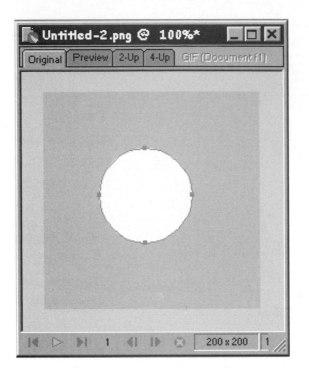

3. If you don't already have the Fill panel open, go to Window ➤ Stroke, or use the shortcut Shift+F7.

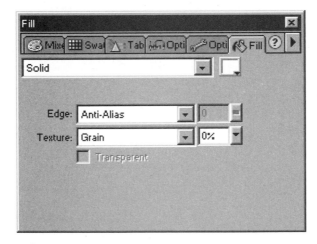

Because the default fill category is Solid, we're going to move on and look at how you can change the color of the fill from the default white to something else. If you want to experiment with some of the other types of fills, explore them using the Fill Category drop-down menu.

Choosing a Fill Color

To change the color of the fill, follow these steps:

1. With the Fill panel open and the ellipse selected, click the color swatch (which should currently be white) to open the Color Palette.

2. With the Color Palette open, move your cursor (which is now in the form of an eyedropper icon) over the color you desire and click your mouse button. For our purposes, click the bright green color in the upper right-hand corner of the Color Palette. Notice that the fill of the ellipse automatically changes to the green you selected.

Note

If you aren't happy with the available colors, you can mix your own with the Color dialog box. For step-by-step instructions on how to mix your own fill color with the Color dialog box, flip back to the section in this chapter titled "Changing the Stroke color."

Working with the Fill Edge

Fireworks offers you three choices for setting the characteristic of the fill edge: hard edge, feathered edge, and anti-aliased edge.

Anti-aliasing smoothes jagged edges that may occur on rounded objects, such as ellipses and circles, by blending the edge into the background. (By default, fill edges are anti-aliased.) Feathering, on the other hand, creates an obvious blend on either side of the edge that results in a softened effect—almost a glow.

For our purposes, we'll take the ellipse we've been working with and learn step-by-step how to feather the edges of an object. For this example, change the ellipse's fill color to something other than white. A document background set to transparent is good, as we want the object to stand out (a white object with feathered edges can easily get lost in a transparent document background).

Anti-aliasing

In graphic design, aliasing occurs when a computer monitor, printer, or graphics file does not have a high enough resolution to represent a graphic image or text. An aliased image is often said to have the "jaggies." On the other hand, an anti-aliased image's edges are blended slightly into the background to create the illusion of a smooth edge.

235

1. Select Feather from the Edge drop-down menu.

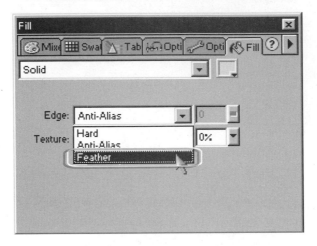

2. Once you've chosen Feather, notice that the field directly to the right of the Edge drop-down menu becomes active. The number in this field represents the feathering amount (in pixels) of the object (in our case, the ellipse). A higher number will make the edge of the object more diffuse, while a lower number will make it less diffuse.

3. Type **25** in the Amount of Feather field and hit Enter. You can alternatively use the Amount of Feather slider (which is accessible by clicking the small down-pointing arrow just to the right of the field) to manually adjust the value.

4. You'll notice that the edges of the ellipse diffuse, automatically reacting to your changes.

[Screenshot: Untitled-2.png @ 100%* window with Original, Preview, 2-Up, 4-Up, GIF (Document f1) tabs, showing a circle with selection handles; bottom shows 200 x 200]

Setting the Fill Texture

As in the case of stroke, you can also set the texture of an object's fill. Lets take a look at how:

1. Make sure the Fill panel is open and the ellipse is selected.

2. Choose a texture from the Texture drop-down menu. You'll notice that a small preview pops up directly to the right of each of the textures when you move your mouse over it. For our purposes, choose Microbes from the drop-down menu. You'll notice that the ellipse's fill texture automatically changes.

[Screenshot: Fill panel with tabs Mixe, Swat, Tab, Opti, Opti, Fill. Solid drop-down. Edge: Feather 25. Texture: Microbes 100%. Transparent checkbox.]

You can now set the amount of texture (by percent).

1. Make sure the Fill panel is open and the ellipse is selected.

2. Type a value in the Amount of Texture field and hit Enter. You can also adjust the amount of texture manually by using the slider (which is accessible by clicking the small down-pointing arrow just to the right of the field). The more texture you want visible, the higher the percent should be. For our purposes, set the amount of texture to **100%**.

Summary

This chapter covered some fairly important ground. It looked at working with layers in Fireworks, exploring the nature of a bitmap image, and using the tools for working on bitmaps (such as Bitmap Edit Mode). It also covered vector images and Vector Edit Mode and how to create basic shapes and freeform paths. The chapter concluded with procedures for changing the stroke and fill of an object by using the Stroke and Fill panels.

Chapter 10

Working with Text

Back in Chapter 3, I extolled the power of type as a visual medium. I'm going to say it again, because I really can't express enough how incredibly powerful type is for creating something potent and beautiful. When it comes to the web, where would graphics be without type? Whether it's a button or a photo, text can add that extra oomph that turns a good graphic into a great graphic.

For a graphic program, Fireworks has some sophisticated text tools. In this chapter, you'll use these tools to create and manipulate text. You'll learn all the cool things you can do with text to make it look exactly how you want it. Finally, you'll learn how to edit text after you've created it. Topics in this chapter include:

- Adding text with the Text Editor
- Changing text attributes
- Moving a text block
- Editing text

(In this chapter, you'll use these tools to create and manipulate text.)

Adding Text with the Text Editor

The majority of the work you'll do with text in Fireworks is done with the Text Editor. With the Text Editor you can create, edit, and then reedit all of your text. We'll start off by looking at how you use the Text Editor to enter text in your Fireworks document. Later in the chapter, we'll get to the other options in the Text Editor. So, let's get to it!

1. If you don't already have a document open, create a new one. (Flip back to Chapter 8, "Setting Up a Fireworks Document," if you need to refresh your memory.) For our purposes, the background color of your document should be black (this will make sense later).

2. Select the Text tool from the Toolbox.

3. Click your cursor where you want your text block to begin in your document.

Text block

All text in a Fireworks document appears inside a rectangle with handles, called a text block.

240

4. As soon as you click your cursor in the document, the Text Editor will appear.

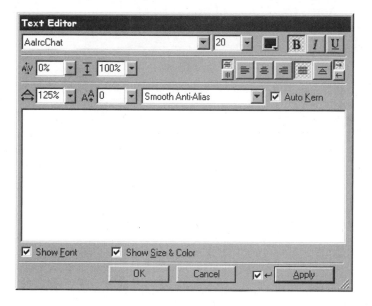

5. Click your cursor in the text entry box, and then type your text.

Type your text here.

6. If you want to see the text in the document as you type it in the Text Editor, click the Auto-Apply check box in the Text Editor.

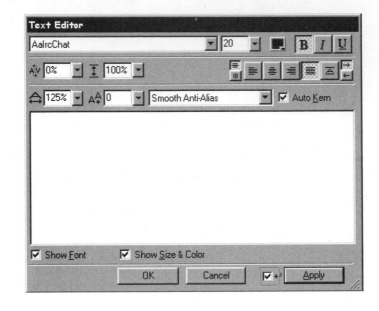

 Note

The default color for text is white. In order to make sure that the text you create is distinguishable, start with a black background.

7. Once you've typed in the text you want, click the Apply button (if you don't have the Auto-Apply option selected already).

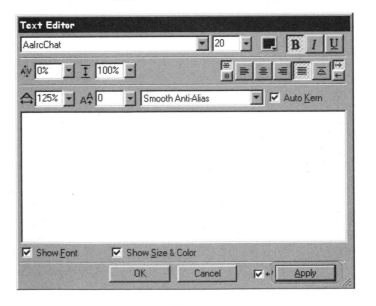

8. Click OK.

If you decide that you don't want to add the text to the document after you've typed it in (and before you hit OK), simply hit the Cancel button. The Text Editor will close without adding the new text to your document.

Moving a Text Block

Like any object in Fireworks, you can move a text block with the Selection tool. Let's take a look at how:

1. Choose the Selection tool from the Toolbox.

Tip

If you have two documents open at the same time, you can use the same click-and-drag method to move text blocks between them.

2. Click anywhere on the text block with the Selection tool. Notice how the text block is surrounded by a light blue rectangular border. This is the boundary of the text block.

3. With the mouse button held down, drag the text block to another location. Note that when you are moving the text, only the outlines of the text block actually move.

Tip

Text can also be moved using the same technique when you have the Text Editor open.

4. When you've dragged the text block outline to the desired location, simply release your mouse button. The text automatically jumps to its new place.

Changing Text Attributes

The joy of text is that it comes in so many sizes, shapes, and colors. It's this versatility that makes it such a powerful visual medium. You can always find a font that fits your need. This font's characteristics can be further manipulated to get it to look *exactly* how you want. When it comes to Fireworks, all of this manipulation takes place in—you guessed it—the Text Editor.

Tip

Because you are creating an image, you are not limited to the system fonts, as you are with straight HTML text. Because of this, you are able to let your creativity run wild with fonts.

Changing Font

Follow these steps to change the text font using the Text Editor:

1. If you don't already have a document open, create a new one. Make sure that you are working in a document with a black background.

Tip

You aren't limited to one font in a text block. In fact, you can use as many fonts as there are letters in your text block if you'd like.

2. Select the Text tool from the Toolbox.

3. Click your cursor where you want your text block to begin in your document.

4. As soon as you click your cursor in the document, the Text Editor will appear.

5. Before you type your text in the text entry field, open the Font drop-down menu. (Notice that a small pop-up box containing a preview of the font appears next to each font when you move your mouse over it.)

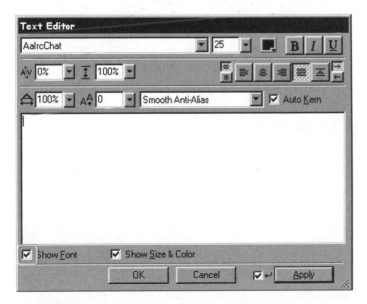

6. When you've located a font that you like in the Font drop-down menu, click it. You'll notice that the font name is automatically displayed.

Note

The fonts available to you in the Font drop-down menu are determined by what fonts are installed on your computer.

7. Click your cursor in the text entry field and type your text.

8. If you want the proper font to be displayed in the text entry field, click the Show Font check box In the bottom-left corner of the Text Editor.

Tip

You can also change the font of text that you've already entered in the text entry field by selecting it and then choosing a different font from the Font drop-down menu.

9. Click Apply (if you don't already have the Auto-Apply option selected).

10. Click OK.

Changing Text Size

Unlike Dreamweaver, Fireworks allows you to size fonts using the traditional point sizes. Follow these steps to change the size of the text you are creating:

1. If you don't already have a document open, create a new one. Make sure that you are working in a document with a black background.

2. Select the Text tool from the Toolbox.

3. Click your cursor where you want the text block to begin in your document to open the Text Editor.

4. Before you type your text in the text entry field, enter a value in the Size field.

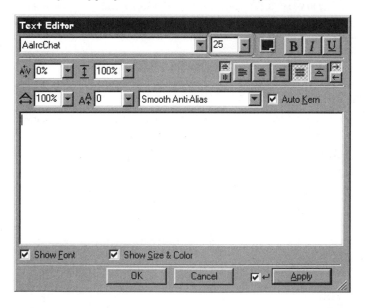

5. Type the desired text in the text entry field, click Apply, and then click OK.

You can also change the size of text that you've already entered in the text entry field by selecting it and then typing a different value in the Size field.

Changing Text Color

Now we're going to take a look at how to change the color of the text from the default white to something different:

1. If you don't already have a document open, create a new one. (The color of the background really doesn't matter for this section.)

2. Select the Text tool from the Toolbox.

3. Click your cursor where you want the text block to begin in your document to open the Text Editor.

4. Click the color swatch just to the right of the Size field to open the text Color Palette.

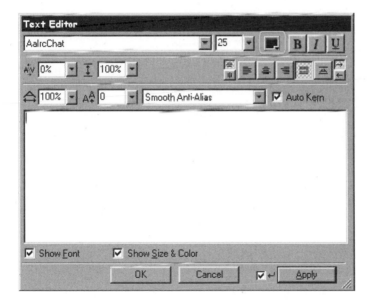

5. Move your cursor (which has become an eyedropper) over your desired text color and click your mouse button. Notice that the color of the swatch changes to reflect your choice. If you aren't happy with the colors available, you can mix your own color in the Color dialog box.

Note

For help with mixing a new color with the Color dialog box, flip back to the last chapter and refer to the sections on changing stroke and fill color.

6. Type your text in the text entry field, click Apply, and then click OK.

Tip

You can also change the color of text that you've already entered in the text entry field by selecting it and then choosing a different color from the text Color Palette.

Changing Text Style

From Chapter 3, "Adding and Manipulating Text," you know that text styles include **bold**, *italics*, <u>underline</u>, and others. Unfortunately, you don't have access to the same amount of text styles in Fireworks as you do in Dreamweaver. Basically, you are limited to the ones mentioned above. On the plus side, applying a style to a text block is a snap. Let's have a look:

1. If you don't already have a document open, create a new one. (The background color really doesn't matter for this section.)

2. Select the Text tool from the Toolbox.

3. To open the Text Editor, click your cursor where you want the text block to begin.

4. Before you type text in the text entry field, click one of the text style buttons in the top-right corner of the Text Editor.

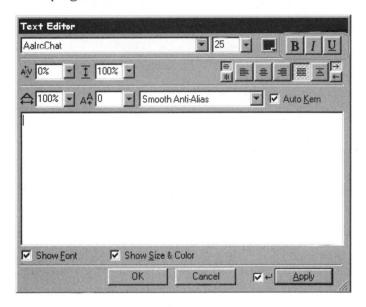

5. After you choose the style (or combination of styles) you want, type your text in the text entry field, click Apply, and then click OK.

Tip

You can also change the style of text that you've already entered in the text entry field by selecting it and then clicking one of the text style buttons.

Aligning Text

When you set text alignment, you determine the position of each line of text in a text block relative to the left and right edges. You can align text to the left,

to the right edges,

to the center,

or stretched so that it's aligned to both the right and left (also called full justification).

Tip

For all intents and purposes, aligning text within a text box has a visible effect only when you have multiple lines of text with different lengths.

Let's take a look at how to set text alignment:

1. If you don't already have a document open, create a new one. Make sure to choose a text color that stands out against the background of your document.

2. Select the Text tool from the Toolbox.

3. Click your cursor where you want the text block to begin in your document to open the Text Editor.

4. Before you type in any text, click one of the alignment option buttons.

5. When you've chosen an alignment option, type your text in the text entry field.

6. Click Apply.

7. Click OK.

Tip

You can also change the alignment of text that you've already entered in the text entry field by selecting it and then clicking one of the alignment option buttons.

Setting Text Orientation

One of the neat things about working with text in Fireworks is that you aren't stuck with text that flows along a horizontal line. You can actually change the orientation of your text so that it flows vertically as well. Let's take a look at how:

1. If you don't already have a document open, create a new one. Make sure to choose a text color that stands out against the background of your document.

2. Select the Text tool from the Toolbox.

3. Click your cursor where you want the text block to begin in your document to open the Text Editor.

4. Before you type in any text, click either the Horizontal Text button (which is on top) or the Vertical Text button (which is on the bottom).

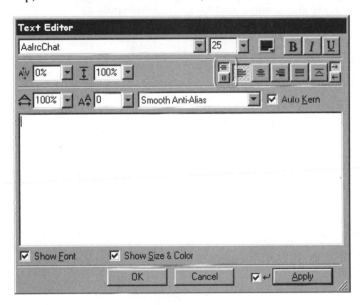

5. Once you've chosen an orientation option, type your text in the text entry field, click Apply, and then click OK.

Tip

To change the alignment of text that you've already entered in the text entry field, select it and then click one of the orientation option buttons.

Setting Text Baseline Shift

The concept of baseline shift sounds a lot more complicated than it really is. Basically, baseline shift refers to how closely the text sits above or below its natural baseline (the bottom of the letters). By changing a text block's baseline shift, you can create superscript or subscript characters. Here's how to change a text block's baseline shift:

1. If you don't already have a document open, create a new one. Make sure to choose a text color that stands out against the background of your document.

2. Select the Text tool from the Toolbox.

3. Click your cursor where you want the text block to begin in your document to open the Text Editor.

4. Type in the characters **H2O** in the text entry field. Notice that all three characters appear along the same baseline in your document.

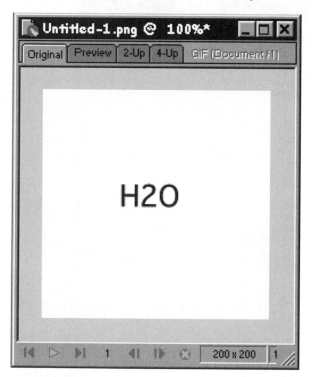

5. In the text entry field, select the 2 in *H2O*.

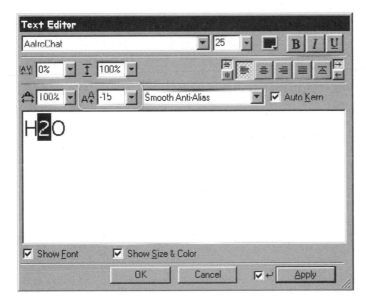

6. Enter **−15** in the Baseline Shift field. You can also increase or decrease the Baseline shift by using the slider (which is accessible by clicking the small down-pointing arrow just to the right of the Baseline Shift field).

Note

A higher number will raise the character above the baseline, while a lower number (the options range from −99 to 100) will drop the character below the baseline.

7. If you watch your document, the 2 in *H20* will automatically drop below the baseline, creating a proper subscript character.

8. Click Apply and then OK.

Setting Text Leading

Text *leading* is the distance (represented by percent) between adjacent lines in a paragraph. A higher leading means the lines will be further apart, while a lower leading will pack the lines closer together.

Leading

Leading is the distance (represented by percent) between adjacent lines in a paragraph.

> **Note**
>
> Text leading can be lowered to such an extent that the lines in a paragraph actually overlap.

To set or change text leading, follow these steps:

1. If you don't already have a document open, create a new one. Make sure to choose a text color that stands out against the background of your document.

2. Select the Text tool from the Toolbox.

3. To open the Text Editor, click your cursor where you want the text block to begin.

4. Enter the number **200** in the Text Leading field.

5. Type in the following: **H20 is** (hit Enter) **really just** (hit Enter) **water**.

6. Notice that the lines of text you just entered in the text entry field are widely spaced in your document.

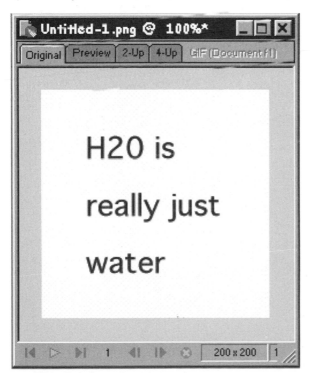

7. Click Apply and then OK.

Setting Text Kerning

Kerning
The distance between characters in a string of text.

While leading increases the distance between individual lines, kerning increases the distance between individual characters. If you have a higher kerning, the characters will be further apart, while lower kerning results in closely spaced characters. To set text kerning, follow these steps:

1. If you don't already have a document open, create a new one. Make sure to choose a text color that stands out against the background of your document.

2. Select the Text tool from the Toolbox.

3. To open the Text Editor, click your cursor where you want the text block to begin.

4. Type the word **water** in the text entry field.

5. Select all the characters in the word.

Text Editor

AalrcChat | 25 | B | I | U

AV 0% | 100% |

100% | AA 0 | Smooth Anti-Alias | ☑ Auto Kern

water

☑ Show Font   ☑ Show Size & Color

OK   Cancel   ☑ ↵   Apply

6. Type **50** into the Text Kerning field. You can also use the Kerning slider, which is accessible by clicking the small down-pointing arrow just to the right of the Kerning field, to increase or decrease the kerning.

Text Editor

AalrcChat | 25 | B | I | U

AV 50 | 100% |

100% | AA 0 | Smooth Anti-Alias | ☑ Auto Kern

water

☑ Show Font   ☑ Show Size & Color

OK   Cancel   ☑ ↵   Apply

261

7. Click Apply.

8. Notice how the characters in the word *water* (in the text entry field) spread out.

![Fireworks document window titled "Untitled-1.png @ 100%*" with tabs Original, Preview, 2-Up, 4-Up, GIF (Document f1); the word "w a t e r" appears spaced out in the canvas; status bar reads 200 x 200.]

9. Click OK.

Setting Text Horizontal Scale

Imagine if you wrote a word on a piece of stretchy rubber, and then pulled it horizontally to twice its normal size. Basically, the word would then be twice its normal width. Essentially, this is what you do when you set text horizontal scale. When you increase the scale, you stretch out the words horizontally. If you decrease the horizontal scale, you squish the words closer together.

Let's take a look at how you set horizontal scale in Fireworks:

1. If you don't already have a document open, create a new one. Make sure to choose a text color that stands out against the background of your document.

2. Select the Text tool from the Toolbox.

3. To open the Text Editor, click your cursor where you want the text block to begin.

4. Type the word **earth** in the text entry field.

5. Select all the characters in the word.

6. Enter **200** in the Horizontal Scale field.

7. Click Apply.

8. Notice that the word *earth* has stretched horizontally.

9. Click OK.

Setting Text Anti-aliasing

By setting anti-aliasing, you can smooth the edges of your text so that it blends better with the background. Your four choices (No Anti-Alias, Crisp Anti-Alias, Strong Anti-Alias, and Smooth Anti-Alias) range from a total lack of anti-aliasing (which results in those horrible "jaggies" we discussed in the previous chapter) to a maximum amount of anti-aliasing. To set the level of anti-aliasing for text, follow these steps:

1. If you don't already have a document open, create a new one. Make sure to choose a text color that stands out against the background of your document.

2. Select the Text tool from the Toolbox.

3. Click your cursor where you want the text block to begin in your document to open the Text Editor.

4. Open the Anti-Aliasing drop-down menu.

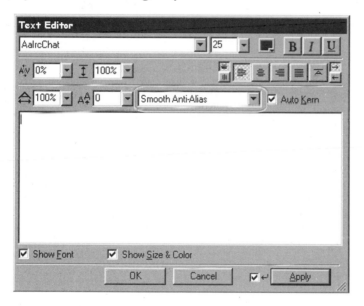

5. Click one of the options in the Anti-Aliasing drop-down menu.

Tip

To change the anti-aliasing level of text that you've already entered in the text entry, select it and then choose one of the options from the Anti-Aliasing drop-down menu.

6. Type your text in the text entry field, click Apply, and then click OK.

Editing Text

Once you've created a text block and inserted it in your document, it's a snap to go back and edit it. Let's take a look at how:

1. Double-click the text block you want to edit, or select the desired text block and go to Text ➢ Editor.

2. When the Text Editor opens, make any desired changes.

3. Click Apply.

4. Click OK.

Summary

This chapter covered Fireworks's text-creation and editing tools. It explored how you add text to a document using the Text Editor and how you move text blocks. It also covered changing text attributes such as font, color, size, kerning, leading, style, orientation, baseline shift, horizontal scale, and anti-aliasing. Finally, the chapter looked at how you can edit text after it's been inserted in a document.

Part 6

Fireworks's Web-Savvy Features

Until now, we've only scratched the surface of Fireworks's true power. As a straight graphics-creation and manipulation program, it easily competes with the some of the established industry leaders. It's far more than your standard graphics-editing program. Although it makes short work of vectors and bitmaps, offers incredible control over type, and has great stroke and fill tools, Fireworks's real strength lies in its web-savvy features. Whether optimizing and streamlining images, creating animated GIFs, or producing JavaScript rollovers, Fireworks really shines when it comes to tackling web-associated image issues. In the final two chapters, we'll take a look at two of the more popular of these features. If you're interested in learning about all the other web-savvy features we didn't discuss here, check out Fireworks's Help feature (Help ➢ Using Fireworks) or check out *Mastering Dreamweaver 4 and Fireworks 4* by David Crowder and Rhonda Crowdwe (Sybex, 2001).

Fireworks's Web-Savvy Features

Chapter 11

Optimizing and Exporting Images

Whether you want to streamline your graphics so that they download faster or pick the most suitable file format, Fireworks is definitely the program for you. It offers a host of tools that allow you to take total control over image-optimization and export settings. In this chapter, you'll learn how to use the Optimize panel to optimize images as both GIFs and JPEGs. You'll also see how to use the Export Wizard to optimize your images and the Export Preview to optimize and export your images. Topics in this chapter include:

- Using the Optimize panel

- Optimizing an image as a GIF

- Optimizing an image as a JPEG

- Using the Preview tab

- Exporting and saving an optimized image

- Using the Export Wizard

- Optimizing in the Export Preview

Using the Optimize Panel

Exporting your images is actually a two-step process. The first step involves optimizing the image, a subject we'll cover in this section. The second step, exporting (which actually means saving it according to your optimization settings), will be covered later in this chapter.

The Optimize panel contains the key controls for optimizing images in Fireworks. With it you can choose the best file format for your image, set format-specific options (such as level of compressions), and adjust the image's amount of color.

Note

Optimization settings apply only to images that are exported. As a result, you can create your image without having to worry too much about optimizing. When you are ready to export, you can choose the best optimization settings for your image and *then* export it. The Optimize panel doesn't actually export an image; it just prepares it for export.

To open the Optimize panel, select Window ➢ Optimize.

In the two following sections, we'll walk through the process of optimizing an image as both a GIF and a JPEG.

Tip

For help remembering the differences between the various web image file formats and what sets them apart, flip back to Chapter 4, "Working with Images," to refresh your memory.

Optimizing As a GIF

GIFs are far more suited to solid, noncontinuous color images. As a result, many of the options in the Optimize panel are related to color issues.

Warning

It's important that you choose the best file type for your image. If you try to optimize and export a complex, continuous color, photorealistic image as a GIF (when it should be exported as a JPEG or PNG), your end result will be an image with horrendous quality.

Setting a File Type

The first, and most crucial, thing you need to do is tell Fireworks that you want to optimize the current image as a GIF. To do this, just follow these steps:

1. Open a document. (If you don't have a document open, the Optimize panel won't be active and therefore can't be used.)

2. If you don't already have the Optimize panel open, select Window ➢ Optimize from the main program menu bar.

3. Open the Export File Format drop-down menu.

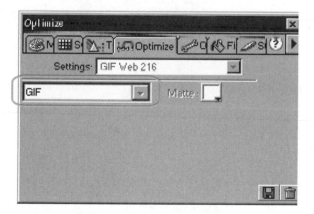

Adaptive Palette

A custom palette of colors derived from the actual colors in the image.

Web Adaptive Palette

An adaptive palette in which colors are switched to their closest web-safe counterparts.

Web 216 Palette

A palette consisting of the 216 colors common to both Windows and Macintosh computers.

Exact Palette

A palette that contains the exact number of colors used in the image. If the image contains more than 256 colors, the palette automatically switches to Adaptive.

Windows System Palette

A palette that contains 256 colors defined by the Windows operating system.

Macintosh System Palette

A palette that contains 256 colors defined by the Macintosh operating system.

4. Select **GIF**.

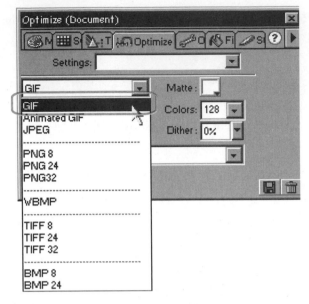

Once you do this, the Optimize panel changes to display the options that are unique to a GIF.

Selecting a Color Palette

You'll remember that GIFs can only display a maximum of 256 colors. This is what makes them suited to relatively simple, noncontinuous color images. Each GIF stores its reference colors in what is referred to as a Color Palette. When you use the Optimize panel to optimize a GIF, you can choose from 10 pre-set Color Palettes. These Color Palettes include Adaptive, Web Adaptive, Web 216, Exact, Windows System, Macintosh System, Grayscale, Black & White, Uniform, and Custom. To select a Color Palette, follow these steps:

1. If you don't already have the Optimize panel open, select Window ➢ Optimize from the main program menu bar.

2. Open the Indexed Palette drop-down menu.

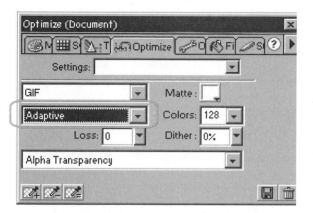

3. Click one of the palette options.

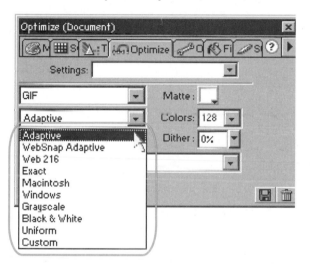

The choices you are faced with when choosing a Color Palette can seem a little daunting, but each has its own specific applications. Familiar yourself with the descriptions provided in this chapter and make the best decision for your immediate needs.

Grayscale Palette
A palette of 256 or fewer shades of gray. Choosing this palette converts the exported image to grayscale.

Black & White Palette
A palette consisting of only black and white.

Uniform Palette
A mathematical palette based on RGB pixel values.

Custom Palette
A palette that has been modified or loaded from an external palette or a GIF file.

Setting the Maximum Number of Colors

Once you've selected the appropriate Color Palette, you can set the maximum number of colors allowed in the exported image. On the surface this may seem a little unnecessary, but when you realize that a larger Color Palette means a larger file, you'll see the wisdom in streamlining the maximum number of colors.

Tip

To find out exactly how many colors are in your image, open the Color Table by selecting Window ➢ Color Table from the main program menu bar. In the lower-left corner of the Color Table, you'll see a display of the number of colors in your image. This will help you make a decision as to the maximum numbers of colors to set in the Optimize panel. For example, if your image has only five colors in it, you can set the maximum number of colors to 5.

To set the maximum number of colors, follow these steps:

1. If you don't already have the Optimize panel open, select Window ➢ Optimize from the main program menu bar.

2. Open the Colors drop-down menu.

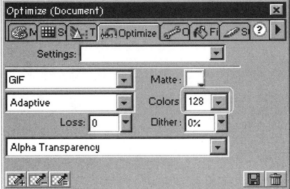

3. Choose one of the preset values from the menu.

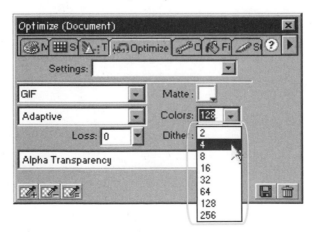

Alternatively, you can simply type a number in the Colors field.

Selecting a Matte Color

When viewing an anti-aliased graphic with a transparent canvas color in a web browser (remember that GIFs can be made so that certain portions are transparent), sometimes a funny-looking pixel halo appears around the edge of the graphic. For native Fireworks files, you can do away with the possibility of this unsightly halo by using the Matte Color Picker in the Optimize panel. To have a seamless transition between the anti-aliased object and the background color of the web page, you should match the matte color of the image as closely as possible to the color in the target web page's background color.

To select a matte color, follow these steps:

1. If you don't already have the Optimize panel open, select Window ➢ Optimize from the main program menu bar.

2. Click the swatch to the right of the word "Matte" to open the Matte Color Palette.

3. Move your cursor (which has become an eyedropper) over the desired text color and click your mouse button. Notice that the color of the swatch changes to reflect your choice. If you aren't happy with the colors available, you can mix your own color in the Color dialog box.

Anti-aliased

The edge of an aliased image is often said to have "jaggies." Anti-aliasing smoothes the edges of the graphic so that the "jaggies" are not visible.

Note

If you need help remembering how to mix a new color with the Color dialog box, flip back to Chapter 10, "Working with Text," and refer to the sections on changing stroke or fill color.

Dithering

Dithering generates colors not in the current palette by combining pixels from a 256-color palette into patterns that approximate other colors. Dithering is helpful when exporting images with complex blends or gradients or when exporting photographic images to an indexed image format such as GIF. A higher amount of dithering increases file size.

Setting Dithering

At a distance, the human eye merges many pixels into a single color. Dithering is especially helpful when exporting images with complex blends or gradients or when exporting photographic images to an image format such as GIF.

Warning

The downside to dithering is that a higher percentage means that your file size will be significantly larger.

To set the level of dithering in the Optimize panel, follow these steps:

1. If you don't already have the Optimize panel open, select Window ➤ Optimize from the main program menu bar.

2. Enter a value (in percent) in the Dither field. (If you set the dithering at a higher percent, you'll get a higher combination of colors and, thereby, a smoother image.)

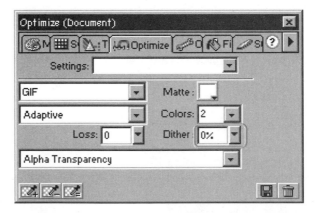

Alternatively, use the Dithering Amount slider (which is accessed by clicking the small down-pointing arrow just to the right of the Dither field) to adjust the dithering value.

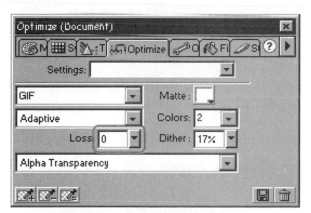

Setting Loss

By setting loss, you affect the quality and compression of an image. A higher loss set-ting (sometimes referred to as lossy compression) means a smaller file size but less visual quality. On the other hand, a lower loss setting (sometimes referred to as lossless compression) means that the visual quality is preserved but the file size isn't decreased.

To set the loss of a GIF using the Optimize panel, follow these steps:

1. If you don't already have the Optimize panel open, select Window ➢ Optimize from the main program menu bar.

2. Enter a value in the Loss field.

Alternatively, use the Loss slider (which is accessed by clicking the small down-pointing arrow just to the right of the Loss field) to adjust the loss.

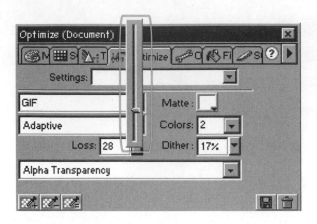

Working with Transparency

One of the important features of a GIF is that it can be made transparent. By doing this, you can make the GIF appear to be a part of the web page rather than sitting on top. Setting a color to transparent does not affect the actual image, only the exported version of the image.

Note

In this section, I'm going to be using a simple image composed of a colored circle on top of a colored square. During the step-by-step process, I'll make the circle transparent so that the background behind it will be visible. You can follow along by creating the same image, or you can create an image of your own and use the same steps.

Let's take a look at how to make a color transparent using the Optimize panel:

1. If you don't already have the Optimize panel open, select Window ➢ Optimize from the main program menu bar.

2. Open the Transparency pop-up menu at the bottom of the panel.

3. Select Index Transparency.

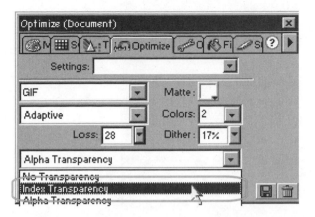

4. Click the Set Transparency button in the lower-left portion of the Optimize panel.

5. Move your cursor (which becomes an eyedropper) over the color in your Document Window that you want to make transparent and then click your mouse button. (In my case, I'm going to click the red of the circle I've created.)

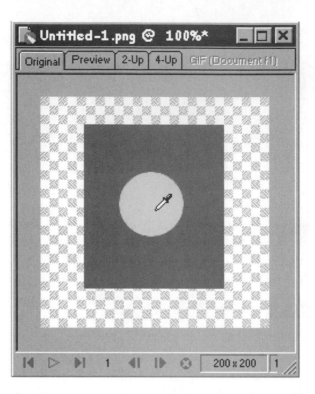

6. To view the image as it will look when exported (complete with the transparent color), click the Preview tab in the Document Window.

7. In the preview, notice that the color you chose is transparent. (In my case, the circular area shows through to the document's background.)

You may find yourself in a situation in which you want to make an additional color transparent. To do this, follow these steps:

1. If you don't already have the Optimize panel open, select Window ➢ Optimize from the main program menu bar.

2. Make sure Index Transparency is selected in the Transparency pop-up menu.

3. Click the Add to Transparency button in the lower-left portion of the Optimize panel.

4. Move your cursor (which becomes an eyedropper) over the additional color you want to make transparent and click your mouse button.

5. Preview the image by clicking the Preview tab in the Document Window.

To make a color visible that you had turned transparent, follow these steps:

1. If you don't already have the Optimize panel open, select Window ➢ Optimize from the main program menu bar.

2. Make sure Index Transparency is selected in the Transparency pop-up menu.

3. Click the Remove from Transparency button in the lower-left portion of the Optimize panel.

```
Optimize (Document)                          [X]
 M ⊞ S ⧋:T Optimize  O Fi S ? ▶

 Settings:                          ▼

 GIF                 ▼    Matte :
 Adaptive            ▼    Colors: 128   ▼
        Loss: 28     ▼    Dither : 17%  ▼
 Index Transparency                ▼

  ⊠ ⊠ ⊠                            ⊟ 🗑
```

4. Move your cursor (which becomes an eyedropper) over the color you want to make visible again and click your mouse button.

5. To preview the image, click the Preview tab in the Document Window.

Exporting As a JPEG

Now that you can optimize an image as a GIF, you'll learn how to optimize an image as a JPEG. You'll remember from Chapter 4 that JPEGs came along after GIFs and were designed specifically to display photographic or continuous color images. Their main strength comes from the fact that they can display millions of colors. In this section of the chapter, you'll take a step-by-step look at what you need to do to optimize an image as a JPEG.

Note

As in the previous section, even though each of the steps that are described has its own subsection, I've approached them as one large process with a number of smaller steps.

Setting the File Type

The first thing you must do in this process is to tell Fireworks that you want to optimize the image you're working on as a JPEG. To do this, follow these steps:

1. If you don't already have the Optimize panel open, select Window ➤ Optimize from the main program menu bar.

2. Open the Export File Format drop-down menu.

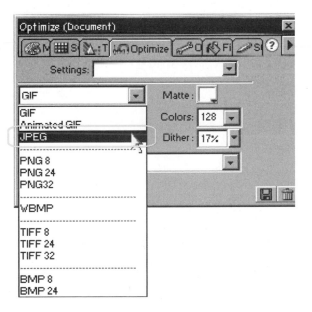

3. Select JPEG.

Once you do this, the Optimize panel changes to display the options that are unique to a JPEG.

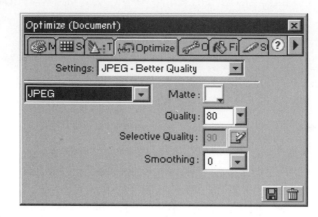

Setting Image Quality

When you adjust the Quality setting in the Optimize panel, you increase or decrease the quality of the JPEG. When you set a lower quality, your image file will be smaller. Conversely, if you set a higher quality, your file will be larger.

To adjust the quality of your JPEG, follow these steps:

1. If you don't already have the Optimize panel open, select Window ➢ Optimize from the main program menu bar.

2. Type a value in the Quality field.

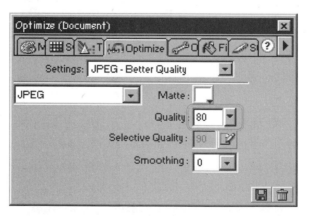

Alternatively, you can use the Quality slider (which is accessed by clicking the small down-pointing arrow just to the right of the Quality field) to adjust the quality.

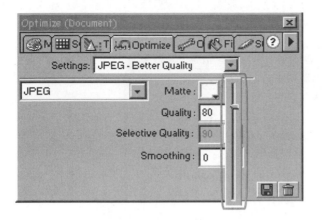

Setting the Smoothing Level

Hard edges do not compress well in JPEGs. As a result, images with many hard edges are generally larger than those with fewer hard edges. This is where smoothing comes in. Smoothing blurs hard edges. A higher smoothing level increases the line-blurring effect and reduces the image file size.

Tip

A smoothing level of 3 (or below) will reduce your JPEG file size while still maintaining a decent visual quality.

To set the level of smoothing for a JPEG, follow these steps:

1. If you don't already have the Optimize panel open, select Window ➢ Optimize from the main program menu bar.

2. Click the small down-pointing arrow to the right of the Smoothing field to open the Smoothing drop-down menu.

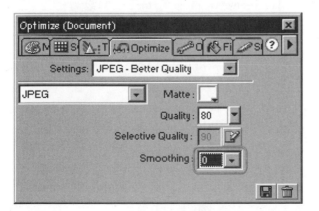

3. Choose a value (0–8).

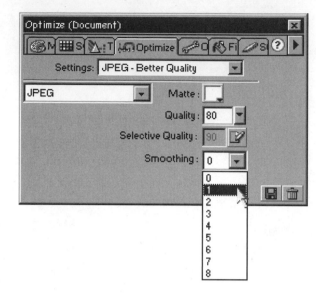

Exporting and Saving an Optimized Image

Now that you've gone through the arduous process of optimizing your image as either a GIF or a JPEG, you are ready to export. When you export your image, you're saving it according to the settings you chose in the Optimize panel.

Note

There are actually three ways to export an image. The first is used once you've optimized your settings with the Optimize panel. The other two, which employ the Export Wizard and the Export Preview, will be discussed later in this chapter.

To export an image that has already been optimized with the Optimize panel, follow these steps:

1. Select File ➤ Export from the main program menu bar, or use the shortcut Command+Shift+R (Macintosh) or Ctrl+Shift+R (Windows).

Note

The graphic here is for Windows users only. However, the process is exactly the same for you Mac users even though it *looks* different.

2. When the file navigation screen appears, type a name in the Filename field. Don't include any kind of extension (like .jpg or .gif) when you type in the filename; Fireworks will add the appropriate extensions based on the file types you chose in the Optimize panel.

3. After you've typed in a filename, navigate to the area on your hard drive where you want the file to be saved and click the Save button.

Using the Export Wizard

By prompting you with a series of questions about the image's intended use, the Export Wizard effectively wraps up the optimization and export process in one simple step-by-step procedure. To take advantage of the Export Wizard, follow these steps:

1. Go to File ➢ Export Wizard. A screen like this will appear.

```
┌─ Export Wizard ──────────────────────────────── ✕ ─┐
│ ┌─ The Export Wizard helps you: ──────────────────┐ │
│ │                                                 │ │
│ │    Select an export format.                     │ │
│ │                                                 │ │
│ │    Find ways to minimize the size and maximize  │ │
│ │    the quality of your image after you select   │ │
│ │    an export format.                            │ │
│ │                                                 │ │
│ │    Reduce file to a requested target size.      │ │
│ │                                                 │ │
│ └─────────────────────────────────────────────────┘ │
│ ┌─ Which do you want to do now? ──────────────────┐ │
│ │  ⦿ Select an export format.                     │ │
│ │  ○ Analyze current format settings.             │ │
│ └─────────────────────────────────────────────────┘ │
│    ☐ Target export file size:                        │
│    │0    │ k                                         │
│                          [ Continue ]  [ Cancel ]    │
└─────────────────────────────────────────────────────┘
```

2. In order to get Fireworks to choose an appropriate file format for you, make sure the first radio button is checked.

```
┌─ Export Wizard ──────────────────────────────── ✕ ─┐
│ ┌─ The Export Wizard helps you: ──────────────────┐ │
│ │                                                 │ │
│ │    Select an export format.                     │ │
│ │                                                 │ │
│ │    Find ways to minimize the size and maximize  │ │
│ │    the quality of your image after you select   │ │
│ │    an export format.                            │ │
│ │                                                 │ │
│ │    Reduce file to a requested target size.      │ │
│ │                                                 │ │
│ └─────────────────────────────────────────────────┘ │
│ ┌─ Which do you want to do now? ──────────────────┐ │
│ │  ⦿ Select an export format.                     │ │
│ │  ○ Analyze current format settings.             │ │
│ └─────────────────────────────────────────────────┘ │
│    ☐ Target export file size:                        │
│    │0    │ k                                         │
│                          [ Continue ]  [ Cancel ]    │
└─────────────────────────────────────────────────────┘
```

3. To set a target export size for your image, first check the Target Export File Size box in the bottom-left corner of the initial Export Wizard screen.

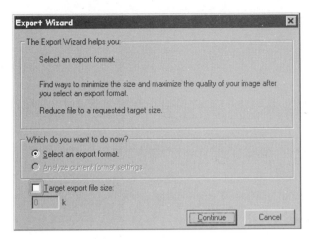

Then enter a value (in kilobytes) in the Export File Size field.

4. Click Continue.

5. After clicking Continue, you will see a screen like this.

6. Here you will need to click the option which best describes the intended destination of your image.

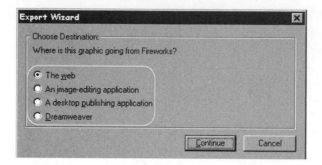

7. After deciding whether you want your image to be exported in a format suitable for the web, an image-editing program (like Adobe Photoshop), a desktop publishing application (Like Adobe PageMaker, Adobe InDesign, or Quark Xpress), or Dreamweaver, click Continue.

8. After several seconds, the Analysis Results screen will appear. Here you'll see Fireworks's recommendations.

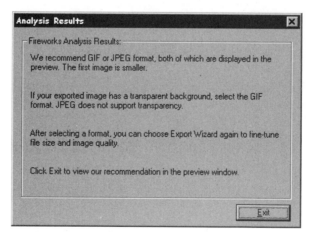

9. When you have read the recommendations, click Exit.

   Fireworks will automatically open the Export Preview screen. From here, you'll be able to tweak the export settings and export your image.

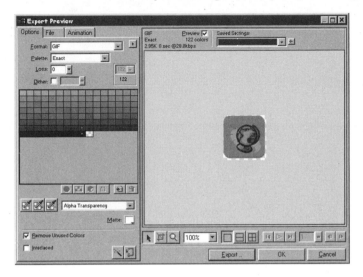

Optimizing and Exporting in the Export Preview

The Export Preview screen is a combination of the Document Window's Preview screen (which is accessible by clicking the Preview tab) and the Optimize panel. With it, you can customize all optimization settings, view the image as it will appear when exported according to your settings, and export the image.

Tip

In the Export Preview screen, up to four possible export previews can be viewed, each with specific information about file size and download time. This allows you to view and manipulate a number of export possibilities, and make the best choice for your needs. To take advantage of this feature, click the particular export preview you want to work with and manipulate its optimization settings.

Let's take a look at how to use the Export Preview:

1. Open the Export Preview by selecting File ➢ Export Preview, or by using the shortcut Cmd/Ctrl+Shift+X.

2. Choose a file type from the Format drop-down menu.

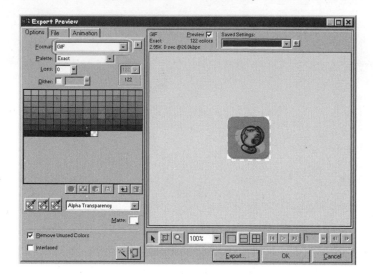

3. As in the case of the Optimize panel, once you select a file format, you gain access to specific optimization settings.

4. Make any changes to the optimization settings. (If you can't remember exactly what this entails, flip back to the section in this chapter titled "Using the Optimize Panel.")

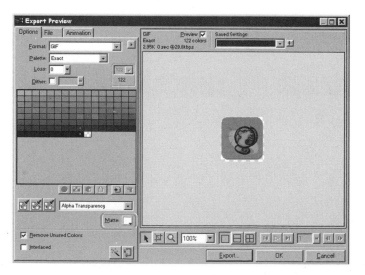

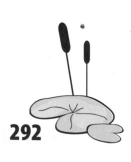

You'll notice that after you set the image's optimize settings, the Export Preview changes according to the changes you make. To view, compare, and manipulate separate export previews, follow these steps:

1. If you don't already have the Export Preview open, select File ➤ Export Preview, or use the shortcut Cmd/Ctrl+Shift+X.

2. Click one of the Split-View buttons (1 preview window, 2 preview windows, or 4 preview windows) at the bottom of the Export Preview.

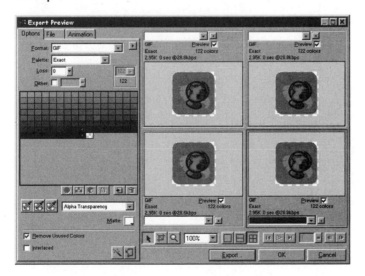

3. The preview area immediately splits up according to the button you selected in step 2.

4. Click the preview frame whose optimization settings you want to adjust. The selected preview frame is highlighted by a black border.

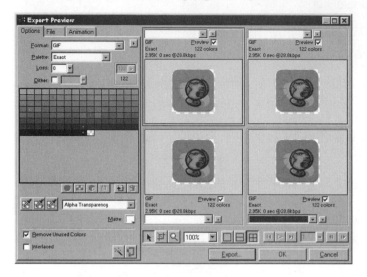

5. Adjust the optimization settings (file type, etc.). The image in the selected frame will automatically change to reflect the new settings.

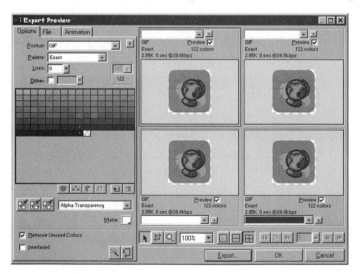

Now that you've made changes to the optimization settings, you are ready to export your image:

1. Click the Export button.

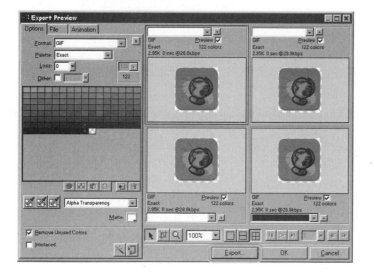

2. When the file navigation screen appears, enter a name in the Filename field, locate the area on your hard drive you want to save the file, and click the Save button (just to the right of the Filename field).

Note

If you have multiple preview frames visible, the one you have selected will export.

Summary

This chapter explored the various tools you can use to optimize and export your images. It looked at how you use the Optimize panel to export both GIFs and JPEGs. Finally, it closed with a look at how you export your image (with the Export Wizard or Export Preview) after it's been optimized. There are some aspects of optimizing and exporting that go beyond the scope of this book. For a more thorough and detailed perspective, I recommend Sybex's *Mastering Dreamweaver 4 and Fireworks 4* by David Crowder and Rhonda Crowder.

Chapter 12

Creating GIF Animations

In Chapter 4, "Working with Images," you learned that multiple GIFs could be combined into one file, creating a digital flip book effect. These files, called animated GIFs, add an exciting kick to your web site. You can animate anything from a ball bouncing across a white background to your company's mascot. In this chapter, you'll take a look at how to create a frame-by-frame animation using the Frames panel. You'll then explore how to use symbols and instances in the animation process. Finally, you'll learn how to loop, preview, and export your animation.

- Creating a frame-by-frame animation using the Frames panel

- Animating with symbols and instances

- Previewing an animation

- Exporting an animation

Creating a Frame-by-Frame Animation Using the Frames Panel

A GIF animation is composed of many different still images that combine into one file that has almost the same properties as a regular GIF file. The only real difference is that when you view an animated GIF with a browser, it plays the still images in sequences, thereby creating the animation.

Note

An animated GIF is inserted into a Dreamweaver document the same way you'd insert a regular GIF. There is nothing special about the process.

To better understand how an animated GIF works, we can use a motion picture analogy. Say that you have a film reel from your favorite film. The film itself is made up of a strip of many frames that each contain one still image. You can think of the film reel itself as a GIF file, while the frames are the individual images that make up the animated GIF.

When you create an animated GIF in Fireworks, the individual still images are made by successively adding frames (and content) to your animation with the Frames panel. The Frames panel lets you add frames, delete frames, set the animation looping, and control a series of animation properties. To access the Frames panel, select Windows ➢ Frames from the main program drop-down menu, or use the shortcut Shift+F2.

In this section of the chapter, we'll take a step-by-step approach in order to create an animated GIF with the Frames panel. In our example, we'll be creating an animation of a circle moving from one side of the Document Window to the other. It's not particularly sophisticated, but it will teach you the necessary skills to create something more complicated and interesting.

Adding Frames to the Animation

The first step in creating our marvelous moving circle animation is to add a frame to our animation and then draw whatever we want in that frame (in our case, a simple circle). Let's take a look:

1. If you don't already have the Frames panel open, select Windows ➤ Frames from the main program drop-down menu, or use the shortcut Shift+F2.

2. Notice that when you open the Frames panel, there is already one frame created. We'll start working with this frame before we add any additional frames.

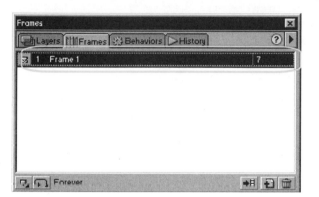

3. Make sure you have a new document open. (I've created one that is 200x200 pixels with a black background.)

4. Click Frame 1 in the Frames panel to select it. Notice that the selected frame is highlighted in blue.

5. Now we're ready to add content (in our case, a simple circle) to the frame. With Frame 1 selected, draw a small circle on the left edge of the document with the Ellipse tool.

Note

If you forget how to use the Ellipse tool, thumb back to Chapter 9, "Creating and Manipulating Images," to refresh your memory.

Frame

A frame is one still image in an animation. The entire animation is composed of a series of frames that play consecutively and, therefore, create the illusion of movement.

After you've added a small circle to Frame 1, your document should look something like this.

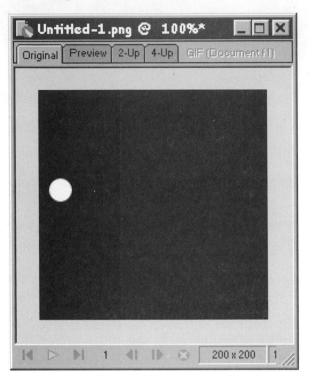

Pat yourself on the back; you've just taken your first step on the road to creating a fantastic moving circle animation. From this point on, the process of adding more frames to your animation is just a repetition of what you just accomplished:

1. With the Frames panel open, click the New/Duplicate Frames button.

2. Once you do this, an additional frame (aptly named Frame 2) automatically appears after Frame 1.

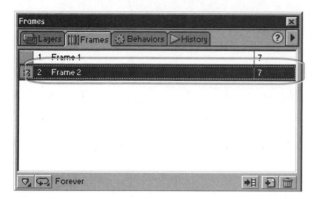

3. Click Frame 2 in the Frames panel to select it. Notice that the selected frame is highlighted in blue.

Note

You'll notice that when you select Frame 2, the white circle that you created in Frame 1 has disappeared. Don't worry; you've done nothing wrong. Each time you create a new frame, it starts off as a blank slate. It's up to you to add the necessary content to the new frame.

4. Draw a small circle (of comparable size) in the left side of the document with the Ellipse tool. You'll want the circle to be a little to the right of the circle in Frame 1.

Tip

You can check the exact position of the first circle you drew by clicking Frame 1.

Now that you know how to create a series of individual frames in which the circle moves a little more to the right in each, you can successfully create the entire series of frames that will make up the fantastic moving circle animation. You'll simply need to repeat the process described above until the circle is at the right edge of the Document Window. In the end, your Frames panel will have a number of individual frames in it. After I was done with it, my moving circle animation had 10 frames in it.

Tip

If you don't want to redraw the same circle over and over again, simply copy the one in Frame 1 (by clicking it and selecting Edit ➢ Copy from the main program drop-down menu) and then paste it in successive frames (by selecting Edit ➢ Paste from the main program drop-down menu). This will also ensure that your circle is the same size as the ones in the previous frames.

If you want to see how your animation looks, flip forward to the "Previewing an Animation" section in this chapter.

Spacing the Animation

It's totally up to you how far apart you space the circles in each of the frames. If you move the circle only a tiny bit to the right in each frame, your animation will have many more frames than if you moved the circle a greater distance. An animation in which the circles are closer together from frame to frame will be smoother than one where the circles are spaced farther apart.

Deleting a Frame from the Animation

You might find yourself in a situation in which you want to delete some of the frames you've just added. Deleting a frame is actually a simple process:

1. Select the frame you want to delete by clicking it in the Frames panel.

2. With the frame selected, click the Delete Frame button in the bottom-right corner of the Frames panel.

Frames panel showing:

1	Frame 1	7
2	Frame 2	7
3	Frame 3	7
4	Frame 4	7
5	Frame 5	7
6	Frame 6	7
7	Frame 7	7
8	Frame 8	7
9	Frame 9	7
10	Frame 10	7

Forever

Warning

When you use the Delete Frame button, you don't get any kind of prompt asking you if you really want to delete that frame. Be absolutely sure you are doing what you want to before you hit the Delete Frame button.

3. The frame automatically disappears from the Frames panel.

Setting the Frame Delay Rate

The frame delay rate determines the speed at which the animation plays. Its value is in hundredths of a second and determines how long that particular frame is visible before the animation moves on to the next frame. One of the neat things about Fireworks is that the frame delay rate is set for each frame. As a result, you can have some frames remain visible longer while others play extremely quickly. In this section, we'll use our fantastic moving circle animation that we created in the previous section of the chapter to show how to increase the overall animation speed. Let's take a look at the process:

1. Select all of the frames in the Frames panel.

Tip

To select more than one frame, hold down Command (Macintosh) or Ctrl (Windows) and click each frame you want to include in your selection.

2. Click the small right-pointing arrow in the top-right corner of the Frames panel to open the Frames panel Options pop-up menu.

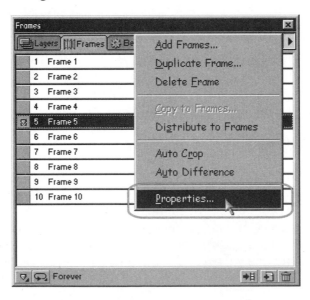

3. Choose Properties from the Options pop-up menu to open the Frame Properties dialog box.

If you set a higher frame delay rate for all your frames, your animation will run slower. Decreasing the frame delay rate will make the animation run faster. If you enter 50 in the Frame Delay field, for example, this means that your frame will play for a half of a second. On the other hand, if you enter 300, your frame will play for 3 seconds.

4. In the Frame Properties dialog box, enter a value in the Frame Delay field.

5. To apply your changes, either hit Enter or click your mouse anywhere off of the Frame Properties dialog box.

6. The change you made is reflected in the right side of each of the frames in the Frames panel.

If you want to see how your animation looks after you've made a change to the frame delay rate, flip forward to the "Previewing an Animation" section in this chapter.

Using the Onion-Skinning Feature

When you were creating the fantastic moving circle animation, you had to create a new circle in each frame without having a precise way to know exactly where you placed the circle in the preceding frame. This was a little frustrating, because, without a way to get the circle exactly in line with the one in the previous frame, your animation could look a little jumpy.

This is where onion skinning comes in. Onion skinning lets you see the contents of frames preceding and following the currently selected frame. With this feature, you can do away with the guesswork inherent in flipping back and forth to see the contents of previous frames and smoothly animate a moving object.

Note

The term "onion skinning" comes from the traditional pen-and-paper animation technique of using tracing paper to view a sequence of animation frames.

In this section, we'll use the fantastic moving circle animation that's already been created to illustrate the onion-skinning feature:

1. In the Frames panel, click the Onion-Skinning button to open the Onion-Skinning options drop-down menu.

Onion skinning

A process by which you are able to view either the contents of frames preceding and following the currently selected frame or all the frames in the animation.

		Frames		
	1	Frame 1		7
	2	Frame 2		7
	3	Frame 3		7
	4	Frame 4		7
⊠	5	Frame 5		7
	6	Frame 6		7
	7	Frame 7		7
	8	Frame 8		7
	9	Frame 9		7
	10	Frame 10		7

Forever

2. Choose one of the Display options. For our purposes, choose Before and After.

Frames		×
Layers	Frames	Behaviors	History	? ▶		
1 Frame 1		7
2 Frame 2		7
3 Frame 3		7
4 Frame 4		7
5 Frame 5		7
6 Frame 6		7
7 Frame 7		7
8 Frame 8		7
9 Frame 9		7
10 Frame 10		7

✔ No Onion Skinning

Show Next Frame

Before and After

Show All Frames

Custom...

✔ Multi-Frame Editing

No Onion Skinning turns the option off and shows only the contents of the selected frame. Show Next Frame shows the contents of the currently selected frame and the next frame. Before and After shows the contents of the frames directly before and after the currently selected frame. Show All Frames shows the contents of all frames. Custom sets a custom number of frames and controls the opacity of onion skinning. Multi-Frame Editing lets you select and edit all visible objects without leaving the current frame.

3. After choosing Before and After, you'll notice that you can see a ghostly image of the contents of the frames on either side of the currently selected frame.

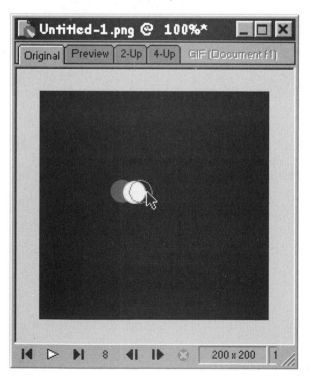

4. To make sure that the circle in the currently selected frame lines up with the one in the previous frame, select it with the Selection tool from the Toolbox and move it to the correct place.

Looping an Animation

In Fireworks, you can control how many times your animation plays when viewed in a browser. From playing just once to looping infinitely (and everything in between), setting the number of times your animation plays is as easy as 1-2-3.

1. If you don't already have the Frames panel open, select Windows ➢ Frames from the main program drop-down menu, or use the shortcut Shift+F2.

2. Click the GIF Animation Looping button in the bottom-left corner of the Frames panel.

Frames		
🔲 Layers 〡〡〡 Frames ⚙ Behaviors ▷ History		? ▶
1 Frame 1		7
2 Frame 2		7
3 Frame 3		7
4 Frame 4		7
5 Frame 5		7
6 Frame 6		7
7 Frame 7		7
8 Frame 8		7
9 Frame 9		7
10 Frame 10		7
▽ 🔁 Forever		➡ ⬛ 🗑

3. Choose one of the options from the GIF Animations Looping pop-up menu.

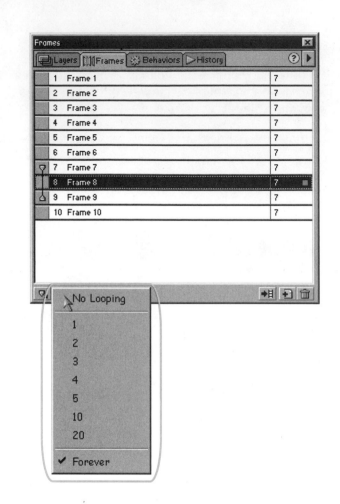

4. Notice that your choice is displayed just to the right of the GIF Animations Looping button.

Frames				
Layers	Frames	Behaviors	History	
1	Frame 1			7
2	Frame 2			7
3	Frame 3			7
4	Frame 4			7
5	Frame 5			7
6	Frame 6			7
7	Frame 7			7
8	Frame 8			7
9	Frame 9			7
10	Frame 10			7

No Looping

1
2
3
4
5
10
20

✓ Forever

Symbol

Any Fireworks object (bitmap image, vector image, text, etc.) that is created using the Symbol Editor, inserted into the Library, and then reused over and over again.

Instance

A copy that is created when a symbol is inserted into a document. Instances can be altered without any change to their "parent" symbol.

Animating with Symbols and Instances

Until this point, we've really only looked at creating an animation by hand drawing the elements in each frame. If you have an animation of any significant size or complexity, this can get pretty tedious. In our fantastic moving circle animation, we didn't run into too much trouble, but what if you had a complicated object (say, a face you painstakingly drew) that you wanted to animate? It would be counterproductive if you had to redraw the same image for each frame. Besides, it would be hard to get the image exactly the same if you had to redraw it each time. This is where symbols and instances come in.

A symbol is any Fireworks object that can be created, inserted into the Library, and then reused over and over again. Each time you drag a symbol out of the Library and insert it into your document, you create an instance. An instance is simply a copy of the symbol that can be altered without changing its "parent" in the Library. By using symbols and instances in the animation process, you can ensure visual consistency from frame to frame.

Creating a Symbol

The first step in creating an animation entirely with symbols is to create a symbol. In order to illustrate the benefits of using symbols to maintain visual consistency, we're going to create something more complicated than the simple circle we used previously.

Follow these steps to create a symbol:

1. Open a new document. (If you don't have a document open, you won't be able to create a new symbol.)

2. Select Insert ➤ New Symbol from the main program menu, or use the shortcut Cmd/Ctrl+F8.

3. When the Symbol Properties dialog box appears, enter a name in the Name field.

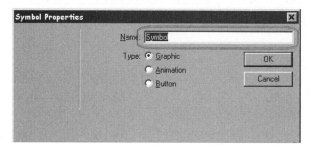

4. Make sure the Graphic radio button is checked.

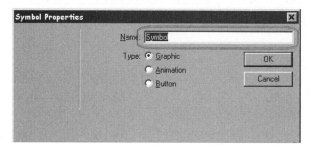

5. Click OK to open the Symbol Editor.

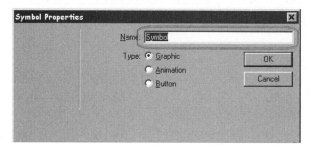

6. When the Symbol Editor opens, draw any kind of object you want.

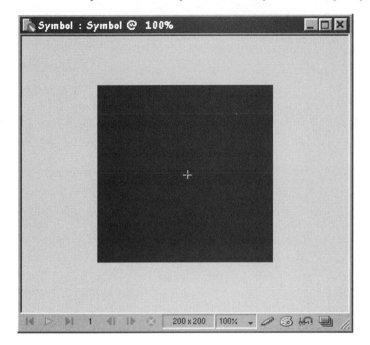

Tip

The Symbol Editor works the same as the Document Window, so you can use any of the drawing tools that you want.

I've simply created a variation on our original circle.

7. Close the Symbol Editor by clicking the Close Window button. (For Mac users, the button is the little square located in the top-left corner of the window.)

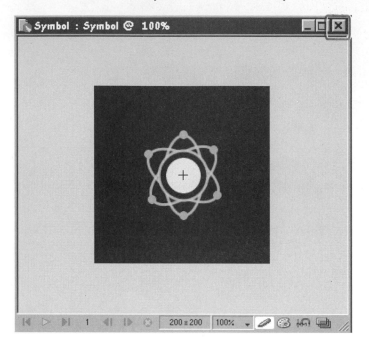

Once you close the Symbol Editor, Fireworks automatically places the symbol in the Library and adds an instance in the center of your document.

Tip

If you've already created an object and don't want to go through the process of re-creating it in the Symbol Editor, you can turn it into a symbol by clicking it with the Selection tool and then going to Insert ➤ Convert to Symbol (or using the shortcut F8).

Symbol Library
The central location where all of your symbols are stored. From the Symbol Library, you can add additional symbols, delete symbols, and edit your existing symbols.

Using the Symbol Library

After you've created a symbol using the Symbol Editor, it's automatically plunked into the **Symbol Library**. From the Library, you can add additional symbols, delete symbols, and edit your existing symbols. To open the Symbol Library, select Window ➤ Library from the main program drop-down menu, or use the shortcut F11.

Notice that the symbol that you created in the previous section is in the Library.

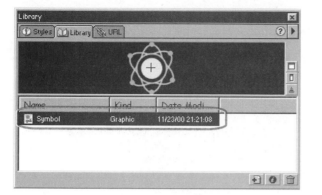

Deleting a Symbol from the Library

To delete a symbol from the Library, just follow these steps:

1. If the Symbol Library isn't already open, select Window ➢ Library from the main program drop-down menu, or use the shortcut F11.

2. Select the symbol you want to delete by clicking it with your mouse. Once selected, it will be highlighted in blue.

3. With the appropriate symbol selected, click the Delete Symbol button in the lower-right corner of the Symbol Library.

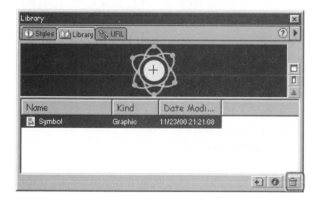

4. When the Delete Symbol prompt appears, click either Delete or Cancel (depending on whether you want to go ahead and delete the symbol or not).

Adding a New Symbol to the Library

To add a new symbol to the Library, follow these steps:

1. If the Symbol Library isn't already open, select Window ➢ Library from the main program drop-down menu, or use the shortcut F11.

2. Click the New Symbol button.

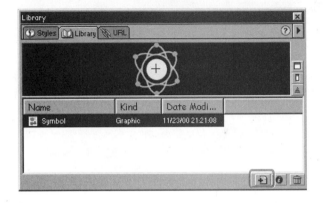

3. When the Symbol Properties dialog box appears, follow the steps that were outlined in the "Creating a Symbol" section earlier in this chapter.

Editing a Symbol

To edit an already existing symbol in the Symbol Library, follow these steps:

1. If the Symbol Library isn't already open, select Window ➢ Library from the main program drop-down menu, or use the shortcut F11.

2. Double-click the small icon to the left of the symbol name to open the Symbol Editor.

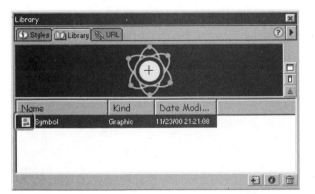

3. When the Symbol Editor appears, make any changes to the symbol using the drawing tools.

4. When you're finished, close the Symbol Editor. The symbol will automatically be altered to reflect your changes.

Note

For help using the Symbol Editor, flip back to the "Creating a Symbol" section earlier in this chapter.

Creating an Animation with Symbols

Now that you can create and manage your symbols, you'll take the next step and learn to use a symbol in the creation of an animation.

In this section, let's use the symbol we created in the "Creating a Symbol" section of this chapter. Then follow these steps:

1. If the Symbol Library isn't already open, select Window ➢ Library from the main program drop-down menu, or use the shortcut F11.

2. If the Frames panel isn't already open, select Window ➢ Frames from the main program drop-down menu, or use the shortcut Shift+F2.

3. Select the first frame of your animation in the Frames panel.

4. Click the symbol in the Symbol Library that you want to use, hold down your mouse button, and drag it into your document. By doing this, you insert the symbol's instance into the first frame of your animation.

5. Click the New/Duplicate Frames button to add an additional frame.

Note

Remember that you can use onion skinning to line up the objects in your animation. If you forget how to take advantage of this feature, flip back to the section titled "Using the Onion-Skinning Feature" earlier in this chapter.

6. An additional frame (aptly named Frame 2) automatically appears after Frame 1.

7. Click Frame 2 in the Frames panel to select it. Notice that the selected frame is highlighted in blue.

8. Click the symbol in the Symbol Library that you've been using, hold down your mouse button, and drag it into the desired location.

   To continue the process, just repeat steps 5–8 until your animation is exactly how you want it.

Previewing an Animation

You can actually preview your animation right in your workspace by clicking the Play button in the bottom of the Document Window.

Untitled-1.png @ 100%*

Original | Preview | 2-Up | 4-Up | GIF (Document f1)

200 x 200   1

To stop the animation from playing, simply click the Stop button (which appears in place of the Play button once you start your animation).

To advance the animation frame-by-frame, just click the Next Frame button.

Untitled-1.png @ 100%*

Original | Preview | 2-Up | 4-Up | GIF (Document f1)

200 x 200   1

320

Exporting an Animation

Now that you've created an animation, it's time to look at how you export it. (This step of the process is covered in Chapter 11, "Optimizing and Exporting Images.") Because the animation you've created is an animated GIF, you only need to be concerned with the optimization settings for export. Follow these steps to export your animation:

1. Select File ➤ Export Preview from the main program menu, or use the shortcut Cmd/Ctrl+Shift+X.

2. In the Export Preview, open the Format drop-down menu.

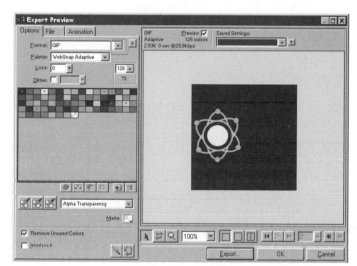

3. Choose Animated GIF.

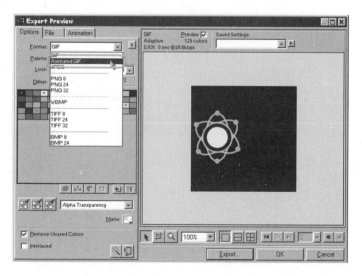

4. Set the palette, loss, dither, number of colors, matte, and transparency options.

For help with setting the optimization options, flip back to Chapter 11.

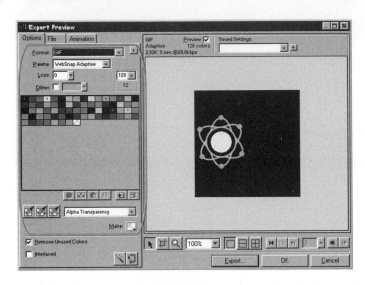

To preview your animation in the Export Preview, use the frame controls at the bottom of the window.

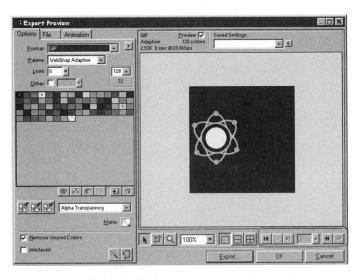

You can also use the Animation tab to set the various animation options (all of which were discussed earlier in this chapter) before you export.

Let's take a look at how:

1. Click the Animation tab in the Export Preview.

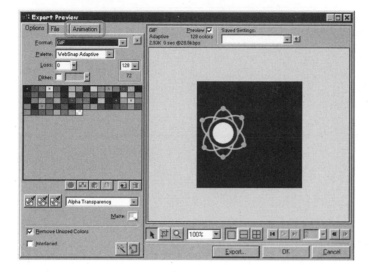

2. To have your animation repeat, click the Loop button and choose the number of times you want the animation to repeat.

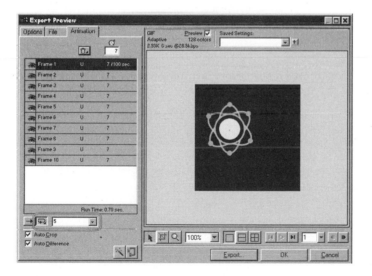

3. If you want your animation to play once, click the Play Once button.

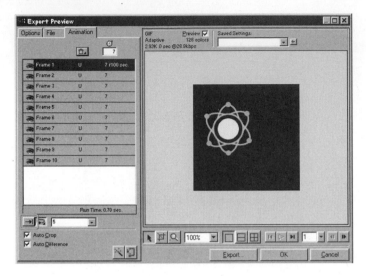

4. To set the frame delay, select an individual frame and enter a value in the Frame Delay field.

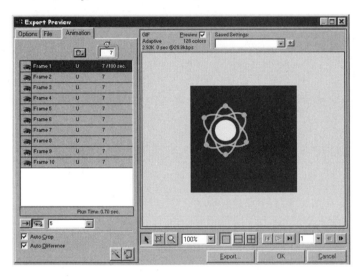

When you're ready to export your animation, just follow these steps:

1. Click the Export button.

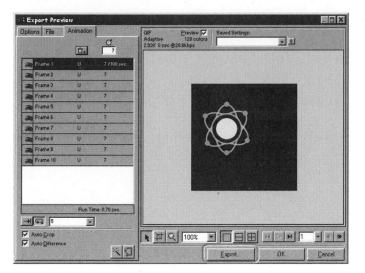

2. When the file navigation screen appears, enter a name in the Filename field, locate the area on your hard drive where you want to save the file, and click the Save button (just to the right of the Filename field).

Summary

This chapter explored how to create a frame-by-frame GIF animation using the Frames panel. It looked at how to add and delete frames, set the frame delay, use onion skinning, and loop your animation. It continued by looking at how to use symbols and instances, how to create a symbol, how to use the Symbol Library, and how to create an animation using symbols. The chapter closed by looking at how to preview and export your animation.

Appendix

Web Resources

This appendix provides a list of useful resources, including links to the official Macromedia Dreamweaver and Fireworks web sites, links to other wonderful Macromedia tools, some other great Dreamweaver and Fireworks web resources, a host of excellent general web-design and development resources, and various inspirational design models. Topics in this appendix include:

- Tools

- Dreamweaver resources

- Fireworks resources

- General web-design and development resources

- Inspirational design models

Tools

This list of useful tools includes the official Dreamweaver and Fireworks sites, as well as links to some of Macromedia's other cool tools:

Dreamweaver   (www.macromedia.com/software/dreamweaver) The official Dreamweaver web site contains a 30-day limited downloadable demo. Also included are hints and tips, links to the Dreamweaver community, and purchasing and product information.

Fireworks   (www.macromedia.com/software/fireworks) The official Fireworks web site contains a 30-day limited downloadable demo. Also included are links to the Fireworks community, downloadable templates, and product and purchasing information.

Flash   (www.macromedia.com/software/flash) Interested in finding out more about Flash? The official Macromedia Flash web page is a great place to start. Learn about the program by taking the extensive feature tour. Get your hands dirty by downloading the 30-day limited demo.

Dreamweaver UltraDev   (www.macromedia.com/software/ultradev) Learn about Macromedia's new visual web-application authoring tool. The most efficient way to build database-driven web application, Dreamweaver Ultra-Dev lets you view code and design simultaneously. Check out UltraDev by downloading the 30-day demo.

Dreamweaver Resources

Check out these great Dreamweaver resources:

TrainingTools   (www.trainingtools.com) This site includes extensive tutorials on beginner, intermediate, and advanced Dreamweaver topics. Despite the fact that they were designed for Dreamweaver 3, you'll still get lots out of the tutorials.

Project VII   (www.projectseven.com) This site includes all sorts of interesting intermediate and advanced tutorials, as well as a host of other tips and tricks.

Fireworks Resources

Check out these great Fireworks resources:

Playing with Fire   (www.playingwithfire.com) This site includes tutorials, examples, and writings that are of enormous value to anyone interested in expanding their Fireworks knowledge.

Project Fireworks   (www.projectfireworks.com) Created by Kleanthis Economou, Project Fireworks features tutorials and how-tos for beginners, a collection of useful extras, and a great list of other web resources.

General Web-Design and Development Resources

Here's a list of good general web-design and development resources:

Builder.com   (www.builder.com) Run by CNET, Builder.com has everything under the sun for the web developer, including discussion boards and lots of great articles and free scripts.

Webmonkey   (www.webmonkey.com) This site has great articles on all manner of topics from beginner to advanced. A definite must!

Techweb Graphics Toolbox   (www.webtools.com/toolbox/graphics) This site is full of great how-to articles and tutorials, plus links to almost every other imaginable web-design and development topic.

Webdeveloper.com   (www.webdeveloper.com) This site includes resources, tech info, daily news, and analytical features essential for the web-development community.

Palette Man   (www.paletteman.com) This great online tool lets you interactively play with different colors and color palettes.

Inspirational Design Models

Looking for a spot of creative inspiration? Check out some of these inspirational design models:

415 (www.415.com) 415 features extremely clean and attractive design as well as a great navigation scheme.

Neostream (www.neostream.com) This site demonstrates incredible (and I do mean incredible) use of Flash to create an insanely (and I do mean insanely) attractive interface.

Northlight (www.northlight.com) The online portfolio of Greg Melander, Northlight features wonderfully clean design with a great interface and magnificent use of colors.

fusionOne (www.fusionone.com) This site has a very clean layout and design that does a great job of integrating catchy colors and cool navigation.

Hecodesign (www.hecodesign.com) This one has an amazingly sleek and sexy Flash design and interface.

Rapidigm (www.rapidigm.com) This site has a very clean design with a great interface.

Circle.com (www.circle.com) This site offers a tight design, extremely usable navigation, and great colors.

Peter Grafik (www.petergrafik.dk) This site shows great use of Flash to create a very playful and visually appealing experience.

Blast Radius (www.blastradius.com) Offering gorgeous eye candy, a beautiful interface, and stunningly conceived navigation, this site is, overall, a mind-boggling experience.

Index

Note to the Reader: Throughout this index **boldfaced** page numbers indicate primary discussions of a topic. *Italicized* page numbers indicate illustrations.

335

341

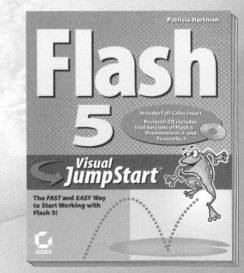

SYBEX BOOKS ON THE WEB

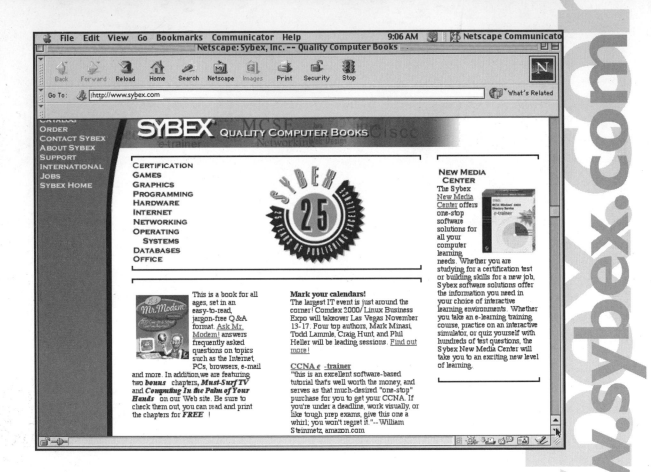

At the dynamic and informative Sybex Web site, you can:

- view our complete online catalog
- preview a book you're interested in
- access special book content
- order books online at special discount prices
- learn about Sybex

www.sybex.com